— God's Creation Series —

GOD'S
WONDERFUL WORKS
THE CREATION IN SIX DAYS

Eric D. Bristley & Edward J. Shewan

CHRISTIAN LIBERTY PRESS

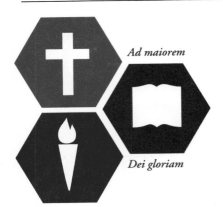

CHRISTIAN LIBERTY PRESS
502 W. Euclid Avenue
Arlington Heights, IL 60004

www.homeschools.org

Christian Liberty Press

502 W. Euclid Avenue
Arlington Heights, IL 60004

www.homeschools.org

Scripture References are conformed to the Holy Bible, New King James Version ©1982, Thomas Nelson, Inc., so that modern readers may gain greater comprehension of the Word of God.

Authors: Eric D. Bristley & Edward J. Shewan
General Editorship: Michael J. McHugh
Designer: Robert Fine
Photography: Digital Stock, Robert Fine, James E. Dau,
        Corel, Artville, Photo Disc
Graphics: Christopher Kou, Edward J. Shewan
Cover Photo: Robert Fine

Printed in the United States of America

ISBN 1-930092-08-3

COVER PHOTO:

The black skimmer is a large, beautiful bird that catches fish while it flies!

Its beak is shorter on the top than on the bottom. This allows it to skim shallows with its lower beak under water. When the lower beak touches a fish, it instantly snaps up. Now it's dinnertime!

— Contents —

— Preface —

Young students need to learn how God made the earth and heavens in six days. The book that follows will help children to better understand that the things that they observe in creation were made by God alone.

When young people study the world God made, they will discover how often nature sings of the majesty and power of the Creator, God the Father. The works of creation continually testify to the greatness of the Lord and inspire true students of science to explore the world with diligence.

The Bible reminds each creature that the fear of the Lord is the beginning of all true knowledge. In this regard, it is vital that young students acknowledge the work of their Creator as they seek to gain a knowledge of the world around them. Great joy and wisdom will flow to all those who are committed to glorifying Christ through a study of the created order.

Michael J. McHugh
Arlington Heights, IL
2000

DAY 1

God Created the Heavens and the Earth

In the beginning God created the heavens and the earth. The earth was without form, and void; and darkness was on the face of the deep. And the Spirit of God was hovering over the face of the waters. Then God said, "Let there be light"; and there was light. And God saw the light, that it was good; and God divided the light from the darkness. God called the light Day, and the darkness He called Night. So the evening and the morning were the first day.

— Genesis 1:1–5 —

1

God, the Creator

The first verse in the Bible tells us,
"In the beginning God created the heavens and the earth."
There is "one God and Father of all" (Ephesians 4:6),
who created everything.

The Bible teaches that even though God is One,
He is three persons: **Father, Son,** and **Holy Spirit**
(Matthew 28:19).

So all three Persons were there in the beginning to create the worlds. God the Father wisely planned the creation to be good. Long before God the Son became the man named Jesus, everything in the world was created through Him (Read John 1:1-3 and Colossians 1:16-17). The second verse in the Bible also tells us that "the Spirit of God was hovering over the face of the waters." He gave power and energy to all the things that were about to be made. **God the Father, God the Son,** and **God the Holy Spirit** all helped to create the heavens and the earth.

Memory Work

Memorize the following questions and answers.

1. Who made you?— **God made me.**
2. What else did God make?— **God made all things**.
3. Why did God make you and everything else?— **God made all things for his own glory**.

How God Created the World

The Bible says that God created the world and the sky and outer space. God made the heavens and the earth from nothing.

Look around the room that you are in. How many things can you name? Now think what it would be like without those things. Before God created the earth, there were no things on the earth. In fact, there was no earth at all. There were no plants, animals, or people.

Hebrews 11:3 says, "By faith we understand that the worlds were framed by the word of God, so that the things which are seen were not made of things which are visible." God spoke and the heavens and the earth appeared out of nothing!

Only God can do that.

Three Things God Created

Genesis 1:1 says, "In the beginning God created the heavens and the earth." From this verse we learn three things: God created *time, space,* and *matter.*

Genesis 1:1	What God Created
"In the beginning"	time
"the heavens"	space
"the earth"	matter

Activity

God chose to create everything that we can see, touch, hear, smell, or taste. Let us praise God for all the wonderful things He has made.

Draw a picture of something you can see, touch, hear, smell, or taste.

See

Touch

Hear

Smell

Taste

GOD'S WONDERFUL WORKS

What is Time?

If you have a clock that has hands that move, sit down and look at it. If you do not have a clock like that, ask your mom or dad to help you draw a picture of one on a piece of paper. Can you say all the numbers on the face of the clock? Watch the hands move on the clock. What do they tell us? They tell us what time it is.

God created **time**. Before God created the world, there was no time. The word *time* means "to divide up." On Day One, God began to divide up each day into seconds, minutes, and hours.

God gave us time so we can glorify Him. How do you use your time to glorify God? (Sing praises to God; read the Bible; memorize Bible verses; pray to God the Father; obey your parents; etc.) Take a moment to thank God for making time.

Activity

If you have a clock with numbers and hands, set it in front of you. How many numbers do you see? (twelve) What do these numbers stand for? (hours) Each hour is divided into minutes. Do you know how many minutes are in an hour? If you look closely, some clocks have little lines between each number. Each line stands for one minute. Count each number and each line between the numbers. How many did you find? (60) This means there are sixty minutes in each hour. Each day contains a total of twenty-four hours.

6

1 Hour = 60 Minutes

What is Space?

If you look around the room, you see many things. Each thing has its own place or space. What would it be like if there were no things in the room? It would be empty. That is what it was like before God created the world. There were no things and no place to put them.

God made **space** on the first day. He made a place for everything. The Bible calls space "the heavens." In space God made a place for the sun, moon, and stars. Look in an encyclopedia or science book under Earth, Moon, Star, or Sun to see what God has put into space.

Activity

If the weather is nice, go outside and look up into the sky. What color is the sky? If you go out at night, you will see something different. What color is the sky? Do you see any stars? The place where the stars stay is called space. Sometimes we call it outer space.

CAUTION: *Never look directly at the sun. If you do, you may become blind. Remember: DO NOT look at the sun!*

7

What is Matter?

As you study about God's creation, you will use this book. Do you know from what material this book was made? Books are made from wood. Do you know where wood comes from? Wood comes from trees. Where do the trees come from? They came from God who made them by the power of His word.

God did not create the trees on the first day, but He created **matter** on Day One. Trees are made of matter. Matter is anything that takes up space. This means that anything you can touch or feel is made of matter.

From the first verse in the Bible, we learned that God made three important things. Can you name those three things? God made *time*, *space*, and *matter*.

Activity

What you need:

objects (feather, pen, dime, etc.); ruler or tape measure; food scale from the kitchen

What to do:

Take each of your objects and measure how long or wide they are. Then take the scale and weigh each object. What is the biggest thing you measured? Which one weighs the most? Is the biggest object the same as the heaviest one? Why or why not? Each object you measured and weighed is made of matter.

What was the earth like in the beginning?

*The earth was without form, and void;
and darkness was on the face of the deep.*

Genesis 1:2

WITHOUT FORM

First, the Bible tells us that the earth was "without form." This means the earth had no shape. Can you think of something that does not have any form or shape?

Water is something that does not have shape. If you fill a glass with water, the water takes the shape of the glass. If you pour the water into a bowl, it takes the shape of the bowl.

The earth was just like water on the first day of creation; and "the earth was without form." Imagine, on the first day of creation, that the earth was like a big ocean of water silently floating in space.

Activity

Fill a glass with water. What shape does the water take? Pour the water into a pitcher, pan, bowl, etc. What shape does the water take? In the beginning, Earth was just like water—it had no shape.

VOID

The Bible also tells us that the earth was "void." This means that the surface of the earth was empty. There were no plants, animals, or people. God created matter on the first day, but He did not make the land, plants, sun, stars, animals, or people until later in the week.

DARKNESS

Finally, the Bible tells us that "darkness was on the face of the deep." There was no light to see what was on the earth. The "face of the deep" means the surface of the waters that covered the earth.

The earth was covered with water. We know this because the last part of verse two says, "the Spirit of God moved on the face of the waters."

How is the earth different today compared to the first day of creation? Today we know the earth looks like a very large ball. It is covered by land and water—but mostly water. The land is filled with all kinds of plants, animals, and people. The earth is also filled with the light of the sun during the day. At night the heavens shine on the earth with the light of the moon and stars.

How is the earth the same now as it was then? If you said it is filled with water, you are right. The earth was covered with water on the first day, and now the surface of the earth is one part land and three parts water.

10

The Spirit of God, Giver of Life

Pretend that you have a lump of clay in your hands. Does the clay move by itself? Now pretend that you are pushing your fingers into the clay. You can form the clay into a round ball. This is what happened in Genesis 1:2.

God had created time, space, and matter, but there was no life or motion in the world. Then "the Spirit of God was hovering over the face of the waters." This means God the Spirit brought life or energy to all of creation. (See also 2 Corinthians 3:6).

What is Energy?

On Day One, the Spirit gave **energy** to the world. Do you know what energy is? Energy is power or the ability to do work. What happens when you jump up and down? You are using energy which helps you to jump high, run fast, or work hard around the house.

The Spirit used energy to form the earth into a round ball and start the ball spinning. Did you know that the earth is not standing still? Do you feel the earth moving? No, we cannot; but it is spinning very fast. The earth spins around once each day.

11

Activity

Here's how to set up this experiment quickly and easily. If you don't have a globe, you could even use a ball to represent the earth.

If you have a flashlight and a globe, you can do this activity. Put a sticker on the globe near to where you live. Place the globe on a table at one end and the flashlight on a stack of books at the other end. Turn off the lights and turn on the flashlight.

Shine the flashlight on the globe and pretend that it is sunlight. As you slowly spin the globe you will see your sticker moving around too. Every turn of the globe equals one full day or 24 hours. When is your sticker in the nighttime? When is your sticker in the daytime?

The earth turns around ONCE every 24 hours.

12

God Created the Light

On Day One, God decided to create light. Why do you think God created the light? He created the light so that we can see. God did not create the sun on the first day of creation, but He did create light.

At night when it is dark outside, you turn on the lights before you start to work or play. In the same way, God turned on the light for us to see. Light helps us to see. Without light we cannot see at all.

When you turn on the light in a dark room, where does the darkness go? That is what happened on the first day of creation, the darkness was chased away by the light.

13

What is Light?

God created a special kind of energy on the first day. This energy is called **light**. Energy is power or the ability to do work, and light is a special kind of power. Light is energy or power that moves through space. But how does light move?

Have you ever been near an ocean or lake on a windy day? The water moves up and down. When the wind pushes against the surface of the water, the water makes waves. This is how light moves too.

Activity

What you need:

bowl of water; eyedropper or toothpick; red food coloring

What to do:

Fill a bowl halfway with water. Let the water sit until it is completely still. Then with an eyedropper, drop one drop of water in the very middle of the bowl. If you do not have an eyedropper, use a toothpick; touch the water in the middle of the bowl with the end of the toothpick.

What happens? The water begins to move up and down from the center of the bowl to the sides. This is how light moves.

Try this again with a drop of red food coloring. What happens? You can see the red waves move straight to the sides of the bowl.

How God Created Light

"Then God said, *'Let there be light';* and there was light" *(Genesis 1:3).*

God spoke and the light appeared!
We should praise God because He is great.
The power of His voice made things
appear that did not exist before.

The Word of God,
who is the Son of God, is powerful.
The Bible also teaches that God is light
(1 John 1:5b).
God not only created light,
but He is the Light of the world

(John 1:9, 8:12).

15

Jesus is the Light of the World

John 8:12 says, "Then Jesus spoke to them again, saying, 'I am the light of the world. He who follows Me shall not walk in darkness, but have the light of life.'" What kind of light was Jesus speaking about?

If you like camping, you know that you need a flashlight to see at night. People who do not know about Jesus Christ are like campers who do not have flashlights. They cannot see in the darkness because of their sin. Jesus came to give spiritual light and wisdom to His chosen or elect children. Anyone who is given the grace to see Jesus as Lord and Savior may begin to walk in the light of God's Word and receive the gift of forgiveness and eternal life.

BECOMING A NEW CREATION

The Bible says, "Therefore, if any man is in Christ, he is a new creature; old things have passed away; behold, all things have become new" (2 Corinthians 5:17). If you trust in Christ, you become a new creation by the power of the Holy Spirit. (Read Ephesians 2:8-9.)

When Peter was preaching, he told the people: "Repent, and let every one of you be baptized in the name of Jesus Christ for the remission of sins; and you shall receive the gift of the Holy Spirit" (Acts 2: 38). If you confess your sins and believe that Jesus died and rose again, you will be saved.

16

God Saw That It Was

Good

Have you ever done something that pleases God? You might say that it is good. God has made many things that are good—one of which is the light. God looked at what He had made and said, "It is good."

God judged what He had made and saw that it was good. This means that it was not evil. When God divided the light from the darkness, He gave us a picture of good being separated from evil.

The Bible says that God is good, therefore, He will teach sinners the way they should go (Psalm 25:8). Since God is good, we should seek to do all things that please Him.

God Divided the Light from the Darkness

When God created light, He did not remove all the darkness. God only separated the darkness from the light. Why did God do this?

God chose to divide the daytime from the nighttime. Since God names the things that He creates, He decided to call the light Day, and the darkness Night. God knew we needed the light in the daytime to do our work, and the darkness in the nighttime so we could rest.

What do you do during the day that you cannot do at night? The light was created by God for us to work. The darkness was made for us to rest.

ACTIVITY

Draw pictures in these squares, showing what you do in the day and at night.

What I do in the daytime

What I do at night

18

Evening and Morning— THE FIRST DAY

"So the evening and the morning were the first day." This sentence is used at the end of each of the six days of creation. Only the number of the day changes. God did not create anything in the evening.

This shows that God worked during the day, and rested at night. Of course, God doesn't need to rest like us. In fact, God never rests (Psalm 124:4), but He stopped working.

Each day has a time when it is light, and a time when it is dark. This means that the earth was spinning on the first day. Do you remember the globe activity? Each turn of the globe equals 24 hours.

Looking Back

Questions

1. Who created the heavens and the earth?
2. Out of what did God create the world?
3. God is One, but He is how many persons?
4. Who gave life and energy to the world?
5. How many days did God take to create the world?
6. Why did God make you?
7. What was the earth like in the beginning?
8. Why did God create the light?
9. What is power or the ability to work?
10. God divided the light from what?

Matching

in the beginning	energy
earth	space
Jesus	matter
the heavens	time
light	Light of the World

Fill in the blank

1. God created the _____ and the _____.

2. _____ made you and everything else for His own glory.

3. Then God said, "Let there be _____ "; and there was _____.

4. Light is _____ or power that moves through _____.

5. And God called the light _____, and the darkness He called _____.

20

DAY 2
God Created the Sky

Then God said,
"Let there be a firmament
in the midst of the waters,
and let it divide the
waters from the waters."
Thus God made the firmament,
and divided the waters which were under
the firmament from the waters which were
above the firmament; and it was so.
And God called the firmament Heaven.
So the evening and the morning
were the second day.

— Genesis 1:6–8 —

God Created the Firmament

After the first day of creation,
the earth had no shape and was still empty.
God needed to prepare the earth so plants,
animals, and people could live.

He decided to make something very helpful
for all living things. Our great Creator
God made the firmament.

WHAT IS THE FIRMAMENT?

This big word means the "sky." The sky is very
important for all living things to breathe and
grow. Without the sky, all the plants, animals, and
people would die.

22

How God Created the Sky

Do you remember what God divided on the first day of creation? He divided the light from the darkness. On the second day, God divided something new. The Bible says that God divided the waters from the waters. He made the sky and placed it in the middle of the waters.

God spoke and the sky appeared, pushing the waters apart. The waters above the sky stayed in one place, and the waters below the sky stayed in another. So the sky or firmament was created by the word of God.

23

God Divided the Waters

After God created the heavens and the earth, he began to make the earth a place where all kinds of plants and creatures could live. He began by dividing the waters which covered the earth. He placed the sky between the "waters above" and the "waters below."

"Waters Above"

Firmament or Sky

"Waters Below"

On the second day, God formed the earth into a ball covered with water—"the waters below." The earth was also surrounded by a layer called the "firmament" or sky. It was filled with air. This is what you breathe when you take in a deep breath. Can you see air? No, it is clear. God made the firmament filled with clear air.

The Bible also tells us that there was another layer made of water that surrounded the sky and the earth. This layer is called "the waters above." It also was clear. Do you know what it was filled with? The "waters above" were filled with water vapor.

24

What is Water Vapor?

Water vapor is like the steam from a teakettle. When you boil water it seems to disappear, but it becomes a gas and floats into the air. Do you know what a gas is? A gas is matter that has no shape and floats in space. This layer of water vapor protected all living things on the earth from bad things that travel in space.

WHAT IS AIR?

Air is a mixture of water vapor, dust, and other things. Air has no color because it is clear. It has no smell or taste. Can you pick it up in your hand? No, you cannot pick it up because it is like a gas. Remember, a gas is matter that has no shape and floats in space.

You can feel the air when it blows on you. You can see and hear what the air does as it moves the leaves and branches on a tree. The air even makes big waves in the ocean.

The air which covers the earth is called the atmosphere. This big word means that the air is filled with many important gases.

Air Helps Living Things

Air carries one important gas which helps people and animals to breathe. This gas is called oxygen. Oxygen helps us to keep warm, build muscles, fight sickness, burn fat, and clean the body. Without oxygen people and animals cannot live.

Air helps plants to live and grow too. The leaves take energy from the sun and air from the sky to make food. This food helps people and animals to live and grow. God made air to help plants make food for us to eat.

Air also helps to clean the water which all living things need. Plants use the clean water to grow and make food. People and animals also use clean water to digest food and change food into energy. Thank God for creating air which helps you in so many ways.

26

What is Water?

You already know that water is a liquid that you drink everyday. Water has no color and it is clear. God filled the earth with water from the very first day of creation.

Water has another name that looks like this: H_2O. This funny name tells us that water is made from two gases: hydrogen and oxygen. Do you remember what a gas is? (A gas is matter that has no shape and floats in space.) When these two gases are mixed together they make water.

We need to drink lots of water every day. More than half of our bodies are made up of water. If you stop drinking water for one week, you would die.

Activity

Did you know that water has three forms?

It takes the form of a liquid, gas, or solid.

Liquid: Fill a glass half full with water. If you tip the glass a little bit the liquid moves with the glass. Try filling other things. Water takes up space but it has no shape of its own. Water takes the shape of the glass, bowl, or container that holds it.

Gas: Pour some water into a teakettle or a pot. Bring the water to a boil. The water turns into steam or a gas. Steam has no shape and floats in space.

Solid: Fill an ice cube tray or plastic container with water. Put it in the freezer overnight. What happened? It became hard. Ice has shape and it takes up space.

27

The "Waters Above"

The layer called the "waters above" was most likely made of water vapor. Do you remember what water vapor is like? It is like the steam from a teakettle. This means that these waters were clear like glass. What did God make on the first day of creation that could travel through things that are clear? God created the light.

There were no clouds in the sky at that time. In Genesis 2:5 the Bible says, "...for the Lord God had not caused it to rain upon the earth." Do you know when the Bible first tells us that it rained on the earth? Rain first came upon the earth when God sent the great Flood that covered the whole earth. (Read the story of Noah and the Great Flood from Genesis 6 through 8.)

The First Rain

After God sent the great Flood, the sky or atmosphere changed. The Bible tells us that "In the six hundredth year of Noah's life, … all the fountains of the great deep were broken up, and the windows of heaven were opened. And the rain was upon the earth forty days and forty nights" (Genesis 7:11-12). This is the first time rain is talked about in the Bible.

When God created the sky or firmament and the waters above, there were no clouds and no rain. This means that there were no storms or lightning either. God had made a perfect world for all living things. This clear layer of water vapor protected life on Earth from harmful things in outer space.

29

God Made the Clouds

After the great Flood, God filled the sky with all kinds of **clouds**. They are made up of water droplets or tiny bits of ice that float above the earth. Clouds show us the glory and majesty of God. One day Jesus will come in the clouds of heaven.

WHAT CLOUDS LOOK LIKE

Have you seen clouds like the ones in these pictures? God made many different kinds of clouds, but we will look at only four kinds. Some clouds are very thin and curl up like a feather. These curly clouds are high in the sky. They are mostly white.

Some clouds look like large puffy balls of cotton. These clouds have flat bottoms and high puffy tops. Usually, they are white when the weather is good. But they become dark gray when it is about to rain. Sometimes these clouds bring thunderstorms.

Some clouds are spread out like a flat blanket, and they do not grow up high like the puffy clouds. These clouds are thick and keep the sunlight from reaching the earth. They are mostly gray and usually make rain. Sometimes they only tell us that rain is coming soon.

Cumulus (puffy)

Stratus (blanket)

Cirrus (curly)

Cirrocumulus (curly & puffy)

30

God Made the Weather

What is weather? **Weather** is what the atmosphere or sky is like where you live from day to day. For example, if you live in St. Paul, Minnesota, the weather will not be as warm as the weather in Baton Rouge, Louisiana, where your cousins live. Or, if you live in Seattle, Washington, it may be cool and rainy, but in Charleston, South Carolina it will be warm and sunny, where your grandparents live.

Do you know how hot or cold it is outside? This will help you know what the weather is like where you live. Is it going to rain or snow? Is it sunny or cloudy? Is it windy or calm? All these things help to tell us what the weather is like. God made these things and they are all part of the weather.

Activity

Make a chart like the one below. In the space below each day of the week, draw a picture of the weather near your home. If it is cloudy, draw a cloud. If it is sunny, draw the sun. Make raindrops for rain, or a snowflake if it is snowing outside. A windy day could have a kite in the picture.

Monday	Tuesday	Wednesday	Thursday	Friday

Water Goes in a Circle

Water is an important part of the weather. The Bible says, "All the rivers run into the sea, yet the sea is not full; to the place from which the rivers come, there they return again" (Ecclesiastes 1:7). This means that the water from the rivers goes in a circle.

First the river water flows into the sea, where the sun shines down on it. When it is warm enough, the water turns into water vapor and floats into the air. Then when enough water fills the air, it turns into tiny drops of water which come down as rain. The rain water fills the land, runs into the rivers, and the circle starts all over again.

Clouds move toward land

Rain Falls

Water turns to Water Vapor

Rivers run out to the sea

Did you know that water comes down from the sky in different forms? It comes down either as a gas, liquid, or solid. When dew or frost forms on the grass or trees, it comes down as a gas called water vapor. When it rains, it comes down as a liquid. When it snows, sleets, or hails, it comes down as a solid.

GOD MADE THE DEW

On a clear spring morning, water forms on the grass. If you go out early, before the sun is high in the sky, you will see tiny drops of water sticking to each blade of grass. This water is called **dew**. Dew is made from water vapor in the air. When it touches a cool blade of the grass, the water vapor forms tiny drops of water.

GOD MADE THE FROST

On a clear fall morning, water forms on the grass. If you get up early, before the sun is high in the sky, you will see tiny bits of frozen water sticking to the glass on the windows. This water is called **frost**. Frost is made from water vapor in the air. When it touches a cool window, the water vapor forms tiny bits of frozen water.

GOD MADE THE RAIN

Rain comes from water vapor that is in the sky. As the water vapor rises, it gets cooler and clings to a tiny bit of dust in the air. As more and more water vapor clings to the bit of dust, it forms a tiny drop of water. These tiny drops of water begin to stick together and form a larger drop of water. When it is big enough, it falls to the ground.

GOD MADE THE SNOW

Snow is not made the same way that rain is made. **Snow** is made from water vapor, but when it is in a cloud that is very cold it changes from water vapor into tiny pieces of ice instantly. This means that the vapor never becomes a drop of

water like rain does. When these tiny pieces of ice join together they form snowflakes. Did you know that God makes every snowflake differently? God is a great Artist and likes to make His glory known even in the smallest snowflake.

33

Climate

What is climate? Climate is what the weather is like in one part
of the world all year long. Weather may change each day where you live, but the climate stays the same year after year. For example, Atlanta, Georgia, has a warm, mild climate. This means that it has warm, humid summers and mild, wet winters.

Climate depends upon three things: (1) how much the sun shines in one part of the world, (2) how high the area is above the ocean, and (3) how much it rains there. The most important thing is how much the sun shines in an area.

The sun shines the most near the equator or center of the earth. The closer you get to the North or South Pole, the sun shines very little. Since this is the way God made the world, what would the climate be like near the North or South Poles? Near the equator?

34

Activity

Ask your mom or dad what kind of climate you have in your area. Remember that climate is what the weather is like in one part of the world all year long—not what the weather is like each day. Pick your climate from the list below:

CLIMATE   **DESCRIPTION**

Cold   at or near the North or South Poles, with very cold, dry weather all year long;

                  or cold and dry during long, hard winters and short summers that are sometimes hot

Warm   cool, wet weather, with cold winters and hot summers;

                  or warm weather, with mild, wet winters and hot, dry, or humid summers

Hot   in the tropics, where it is very warm and wet but sometimes dry in winter;

                  or at or near the equator, where it rains all year round with very hot weather;

                  or in the desert areas, with very hot, dry weather all year

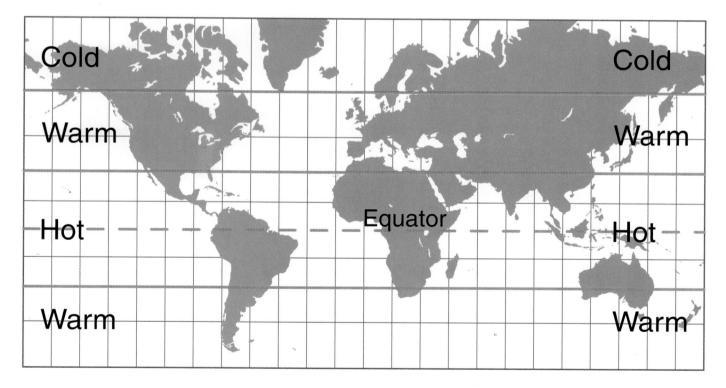

On the map above, find where you live. What kind of climate do you have? The colors tell if your climate is very hot, hot, very warm, warm, cool, cold, or very cold.

35

Looking Back

Questions

1. What is the firmament?
2. How did God create the firmament?
3. Why did God create the firmament?
4. Where did God put the firmament or sky?
5. What is another name for the firmament or sky?
6. When did God first send the rain?
7. What four kinds of clouds did you learn about?
8. What were the "waters above" like?
9. What important gas does air carry?
10. How does water go in a circle?

Matching

firmament	steam
water vapor	oxygen
gas we breathe	sky

Fill in the blank

1. Water vapor is like _____ from a teakettle.

2. God filled the firmament or sky with _____.

3. _____ is what the atmosphere or sky is like from day to day.

4. _____ is what the weather is like in one area all year long.

5. A _____ is matter that has no shape and floats in space.

36

DAY 3

God Created the Dry Land, the Seas, and the Plants

*T*hen God said, "Let the waters under the heaven be gathered together into one place, and let the dry land appear"; and it was so. And God called the dry land

Earth, and the gathering together of the waters He called Seas. And God saw that it was good. Then God said, "Let the earth bring forth grass, the herb that yields seed, and the fruit tree that yields fruit according to its kind, whose seed is in itself, on the earth"; and it was so. And the earth brought forth grass, the herb that yields seed according to its kind, and the tree that yields fruit, whose seed is in itself according to its kind. And God saw that it was good. So the evening and the morning were the third day.

— Genesis 1:9–12 —

37

God Divided the Land and Seas

On the first day of creation, what did God divide? Yes, God divided the light from the darkness. What did God divide on the second day? God divided the waters—the waters above from the waters below. On Day Three, God divided something else. He divided the land from the seas.

God spoke and said, "Let the waters under the heaven be gathered together unto one place, and let the dry land appear." God called the dry land "Earth" and the gathered waters He called the "Seas."

GOD SAW THAT IT WAS GOOD

On the third day of creation, God looked at what He had made, and He saw that it was good. God saw that the land and seas were good.

Why do you think God called the dry land "good"? God saw that the land was good because He had made a wonderful place for every man, woman, and child to live. The animals and plants also had a perfect place to live and grow.

Why do you think God said that the seas were good? He saw that the seas were good because all kinds of fish and sea creatures had a wonderful place to live, too.

God Made the Dry Land

God created all kinds of dry land—soil, sand, and rocks. If He had not made the dry land, you would have no place to walk or play or live. He also made the dry land for all the land animals and plants to live and grow. God is wise in what He does.

God made many different kinds of soil on the earth. Some soil is high, some is low, some is soft, some is hard. The soil may be red or black or brown or yellow or white. All the different kinds of soil are very helpful for life on Earth.

WHAT IS SOIL?

Soil is loose earth that is made up of two things: (1) small bits of dead plants and animals, and (2) tiny pieces of rock. The soil may be a few inches deep, or it may be several hundred feet deep.

Why did God make the soil? He made the soil to help the plants grow. The minerals in the soil help plants to make food. Minerals are things that come from rocks—not things from plants or animals.

Soil gets its color from the minerals in it. For example, red soil has a lot of the mineral iron in it. What is the color of the soil where you live? Why is it that color?

39

Inside the Earth

When God created the heavens and the earth, He made the inside of the earth too. As we learned before, the earth is like a great big ball. Many believe that the earth is made up of three layers called the crust, the mantle, and the core.

The outside layer of the earth is called the **crust**. It is about 35 miles thick. Soil and rock make up most of the crust. The crust of the earth is like the skin on an orange.

The layer under the crust is called the **mantle**. It is most likely made up of very hot rock. At times the rock melts and comes out of volcanoes as liquid rock (magma).

The third layer is called the **core**. Nobody knows what it is like, but it may be made of very hot rock which is very hard. Some people say it is made of iron.

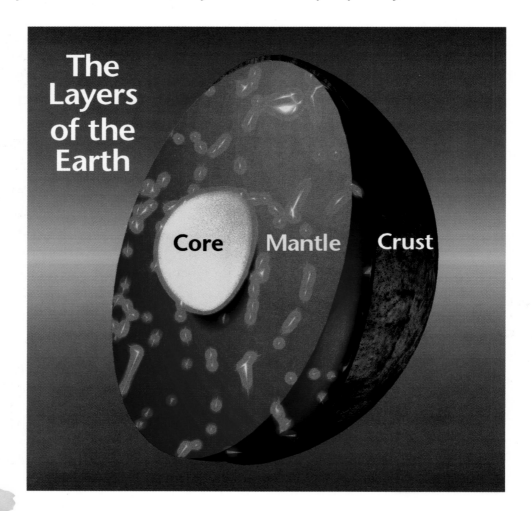

The Layers of the Earth

Core   Mantle   Crust

Three Main Kinds of Rocks

Good created the rocks. Most rocks are found under the crust of the earth. Do you remember what the crust is? (the outer layer of the earth) What material is the crust made of? (soil and rock) Rocks are made up of minerals which give the rocks their color; minerals make the rocks beautiful. God made three main kinds of rocks: (1) fire rock, (2) settled rock, and (3) changed rock.

Fire Rock (Igneous)

The first kind is called **fire rock**. This means the rock is made from hot liquid rock that comes from volcanoes. After the rock cools it becomes very hard with sharp edges. Granite is one kind of fire rock that is made of different kinds of minerals. Granite is very strong and the weather does not harm it. Many buildings are made with this strong, beautiful rock.

Settled Rock (Sedimentary)

God created **settled rock** in a special way. Rain, snow, ice, and heat from the sun all work together to break up rocks into tiny bits. When water flows over the land it picks up these tiny bits of rock or soil. When the water stops flowing, the bits of soil settle to the bottom. The water presses hard on the bits of soil turning them into settled rock.

Changed Rock (Metamorphic)

Fire and settled rocks help make **changed rock**. When fire or settled rocks come near hot, liquid rock, they begin to change. Sometimes they change when they are put under great heat and pressure. For example, if limestone, a settled rock, is put under a lot of heat and pressure it changes into a beautiful shiny rock called marble.

41

Activity

The best way to learn about rocks is to go outside and find some. Take a trip to the country or mountains and see how many different kinds of rocks you can find. If you have a book on rocks, take it with you so you can learn the names of the rocks you pick up.

Collect as many different kinds of rocks as you can find and bring them home with you. If you cannot find too many rocks in your area, you may purchase a "rock kit" from an educational store or through a mail-order company.

Take a box lid or piece of poster board and divide it into squares large enough to glue each rock and write its name. Write the names of the rocks first at the bottom of each square, then glue the correct rock above its name. If you want, you may use other rocks instead of those listed below.

Fire Rocks (Igneous)	Settled Rocks (Sedimentary)	Changed Rocks (Metamophic)
Granite	Shale	Slate
Basalt	Sandstone	Gneiss
Obsidian	Coal	Marble

God Made Minerals

Minerals are things that come from rocks. Minerals do not come from plants or animals. God has formed these minerals into shapes that have flat, smooth sides that meet together with sharp edges and corners. Some have shapes that look like boxes, pyramids, diamonds, or needles.

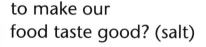

Our great Creator has made about 2,000 different kinds of minerals—about 100 of these are commonly found in the world. What common mineral do we use to make our food taste good? (salt)

Gold is a mineral that is not common, but it is one of the most special minerals that God has made. It is special because it never rusts, and it can be made into all kinds of beautiful things that never lose their shine. What is more desirable than gold? (Read Psalms 19:9–10)

43

Activity

What you need:

a small saucepan; water; salt (or alum);

a glass jar; a long pencil; a piece of cotton string

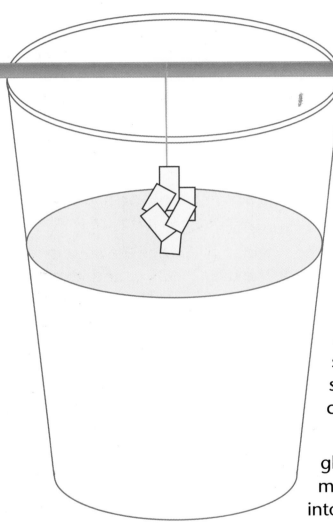

What to do:

Do you want to grow your own gems? Gems like diamonds are costly minerals that have been cut and made smooth. Diamonds are very hard to make, but you can make "gems" from salt (or alum which you can buy in a small packet from a drugstore or in a kit from a nature supply store).

Boil about ten ounces of water in the saucepan. When the water begins to boil remove the pan from the heat and add about one-third cup of salt. Stir until the salt disappears—keep adding salt until the salt does not disappear. Then let the water cool in the saucepan.

Pour the water (not the extra salt) into a glass. Tie one end of a cotton string to the middle of a pencil and drop the other end into the water. Let the pencil rest on the rim of the glass, leaving it in a cool place. Do not touch or move the string or glass for about a week.

After that, start checking the string every day to see your "gems" growing. You can do the same thing with alum; put a little less than four tablespoons of alum in a glass of warm water. After only a few hours you will begin to see your "gems" growing on the string.

God Made the Seas

How did God create the great seas? The Bible tells us that God spoke and the waters under the heaven were gathered together into one place. By the great power of His Word the waters obeyed and were divided from the dry land. He called the waters the "seas."

We call the waters under the heaven "the seas"; sometimes we call them **oceans** which mean "the outer seas." Nearly three-quarters of the earth's surface is covered with the oceans. Do you know how many oceans there are? There are four: the Pacific Ocean, the Atlantic Ocean, the Indian Ocean, and the Arctic Ocean. These oceans are filled with salty water.

Look at the world map below, and try to find each of these oceans. Which ocean is the largest? The Pacific Ocean is the largest in the world. In some places it is 10,000 miles wide! It is also the deepest ocean. The Pacific is more than seven miles deep! Which ocean is the smallest? The Arctic Ocean is the smallest.

Do you think that the oceans stand still? No, they do not. They are always moving. Many years ago, Mr. Matthew Maury was reading the Bible and found these words: "the paths of the seas" (Read Psalm 8:8). So he began to look for these paths in the oceans. He discovered what we now call ocean currents. See if you can find the paths or currents of the oceans on the map below.

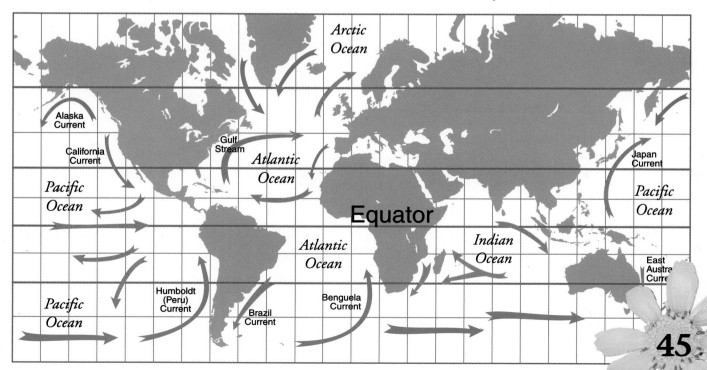

Arctic Ocean

Alaska Current

California Current

Gulf Stream

Atlantic Ocean

Japan Current

Pacific Ocean

Pacific Ocean

Equator

Atlantic Ocean

Indian Ocean

East Austra Curre

Pacific Ocean

Humboldt (Peru) Current

Brazil Current

Benguela Current

Pacific Ocean

45

God Made Fresh Water

God also made fresh water—water that does not have salt in it. The water that fills the ocean, however, has salt in it. The ocean is so salty that people and most animals cannot drink from it. In fact, most of the water in the world is salty.

How does God make the water fresh for people and animals to drink? Fresh water is found in the lakes, ponds, and rivers, but how does God fill them with fresh water? God created a special plan.

As we learned before, water goes in a circle. The Bible says, "All the rivers run into the sea; yet the sea is not full; to the place from which the rivers come, there they return again" (Ecclesiastes 1:7).

Since the water in the ocean is so salty, God created the sun to help take the salt out of it. As the sun heats the water, it turns into water vapor and floats into the air. The salt stays in the ocean, though, because it is too heavy to float into the air with the water vapor. In this way God makes fresh water.

As the water vapor fills the air, it changes into rain which falls to the earth. In this way God fills the lakes and rivers with fresh water. Then this water flows into the seas, and the circle starts all over again.

46

Land Under the Oceans

People who study the oceans of the world have found that the land under the water of an ocean is like the land above the water. There are hills and valleys, smooth areas and bumpy places, deep holes and tall volcanoes.

The land under the waters of an ocean is divided into three areas: (1) the ocean "shelf," (2) the ocean "slide," and (3) the ocean "floor." Almost all the fish that people eat live near the ocean shelf, which is close to the dry land. It is made of mud and sand, and is not very deep.

The ocean slide comes next to the ocean shelf. If you like going down a slide, then you would like the big ocean slide. There are no plants on this area of the land under an ocean, but some fish and sea animals live there. At the bottom of the ocean slide are deep cuts in the land called trenches.

At the very bottom of the ocean is the ocean floor. It has flat places and high mountains. Sometimes there are volcanoes that rise high above the ocean floor; the State of Hawaii is made up of some of these volcanoes. Also, the most interesting fish and sea creatures live near the ocean floor. Many have big mouths, sharp teeth, and some have "lights" to attract their food.

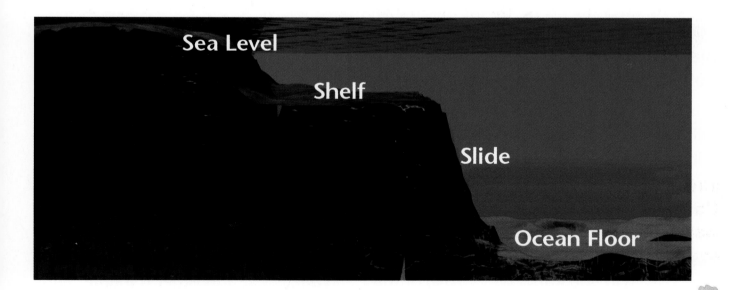

Activity

What you need:

a glass of fresh water; two tablespoons of salt; half of a crayon

What to do:

The ocean is very salty. One of the reasons God put lots of salt in the ocean was to help boats float better. You can do the following test to see how salt water helps things float.

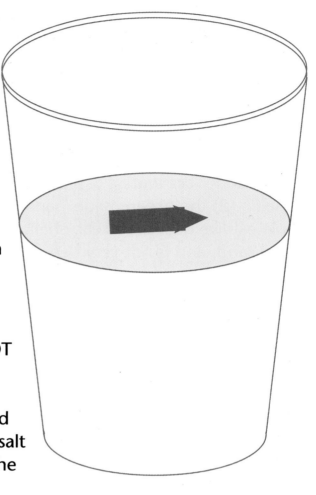

Fill a glass with fresh water. (DO NOT add any salt.) Take half of a crayon and drop it into the glass. What does the crayon do? Now take the crayon out and stir in two tablespoons of salt. After the salt has disappeared, drop the crayon into the salty water. What does the crayon do?

Why does the crayon float? The crayon floats on top of the water because the salt makes the water thick. The salty water has more things in it to hold up the piece of crayon. Fresh water does not have salt in it, so the crayon falls to the bottom of the glass.

For example, if you fill a measuring cup with salt, then a small piece of crayon will sit on top of the salt. If you take the salt out of the cup, however, the crayon will drop to the bottom. Why? (no salt to hold up the crayon) Salty water is like the cup of salt, even though you cannot see the salt. Salty water is thicker than fresh water, so the crayon is able to float in it.

Have you heard of the Dead Sea or the Sea of Lot? It is located in the Middle East; half of it is in Israel and half is in Jordan. In Genesis 14:3, it is called the Salt Sea. Do you know why? 25% of the Dead Sea is salt and other minerals. If you wanted to go swimming in the Dead Sea, what do you think would happen? It is so salty, you would float! It is seven times saltier than the ocean!

God Formed the Herbs and Trees

On the third day of creation, God formed the dry land which is made up of soil and rock. God also made all kinds of living plants. These plants grew out of the soil at God's command. This miracle shows the great power of the Lord.

God is very wise. He made the soil in a special way. God filled the soil with minerals, a little water, and other things that would help plants grow. Without soil plants could not live.

The Bible says that God formed two families of plants: herbs that yield seed and trees that yield fruit with seeds inside the fruit. God divided plants into these two families according to His divine will.

God formed the grass.

God said that grasses are herbs that yield seeds. Herbs are plants which have soft stems. They make seeds that are not covered with soft fruit. Grass includes all the smaller plants that spread out and cover the ground. These include all the plants that make the food we eat, such as barley, corn, millet, oats, rice, rye, spelt, wheat, and many others.

God also formed the trees.

Trees are different from herbs in three ways. First, trees have hard stems, while herbs have soft ones. Second, trees grow fruit that have seeds inside of them, but herbs do not. Third, trees live for many years and form lots of wood in their stems and branches. Herbs, however, live only about six months; then their stems dry up and turn brown.

Activity

Divide a sheet of paper into two parts with a marker. Write "Herb Family" on one side and "Tree Family" on the other side. From old magazines, cut out pictures of rice, corn, beans, tomatoes, apples, mangos, oranges, and papayas. Then glue them on the correct side of the paper.

49

God Made the Grass

After God gathered the waters into one place and let the the dry land appear, He formed the grass. "Then God said, Let the earth bring forth grass…: and it was was so" (Genesis 1:11). By the power of His word, God made the grass that covers much of the earth.

If you draw a circle and cut it like a pizza into three pieces, one piece of the circle would show how much grass covers the dry land of the earth.

Grass

There are many different kinds of grasses. One kind of grass is found in the yard around your home or in the park where you play. This kind of grass is very short, but there are tall kinds of grass too. Bamboo is one kind of tall grass.

People and animals eat other kinds of grasses. For example, the bread you eat is made from grasses called wheat or spelt. The cereal you eat for breakfast is made from oats, corn, rice, or other grains. Cows eat corn and horses eat oats.

God is very wise. He made many different kinds of grass for people and animals to eat. We should give thanks to the Lord for all the good things He has made.

50

The Seed

God has formed the grass seeds with tiny new plants inside each seed. Let us look at one of these seeds. The seed of the corn plant has three parts: the seed coat, the food sack, and the new plant. Each part has a special job to do.

The outside of the seed is called the **seed coat**. It protects the seed from getting hurt. Inside the seed coat is the **food sack**. This gives the new plant food which helps it to grow. The tiny **new plant** is also inside the seed coat. The new plant goes into a deep sleep until it is put into the soil. When it is given lots of water and sunshine, the tiny new plant begins to grow.

Activity

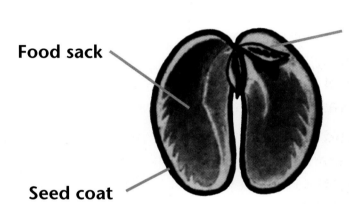

New plant

Food sack

Seed coat

What you need:

dried lima beans; potting soil; clear plastic cup

What to do:

Place a few lima beans in the bottom of a clear plastic cup. Add enough water to cover the beans. Wait and see the seed coat of the beans wrinkle up. After a couple of hours, take the beans out of the water. Carefully remove the seed coat and open the seed. What do you see? Notice the little leaf on the "baby plant." Name the three parts of a seed (seed coat, "baby plant," and food sack).

Empty the water out of the cup and fill it half full with potting soil. Do not push down on the soil. Place a few lima beans around the edge of the cup so they can be seen. Push them down just below the surface of the soil. Add a little bit of water and place the cup near sunlight. Wait a few days and watch them grow. Keep the soil moist, but do not soak it. See what happens each day.

51

God Made the Beautiful Flowers

God made most plants with beautiful flowers. Each flower has a different color. Bees like these colors and come to drink the sweet "juice" that the flowers make.

As a bee drinks the "juice" of the flower it picks up yellow dust on its legs from the center of the flower. This yellow dust is called **pollen**. When the bee flies around, the yellow dust falls on a special part of the flower that helps the flower to make its seeds.

After that, the flower no longer gives off the nice smell that the bee likes. So it goes on to the next flower to drink more sweet "juice." When the seeds are ready, they fall to the ground to start a new plant.

Plants Make Food

God made plants to make food so that we would have something to eat. God cares about us very much. Without the food that the plants make we cannot live. Thank your heavenly Father for all the good things that He gives us to eat.

When God created man He said, "See, I have given you every herb that yields seed which is on the face of all the earth, and every tree whose fruit yields seed; to you it shall be for food" (Genesis 1:29). God gave us good things to eat.

The food of a plant is mostly made through its leaves. Leaves are made of green material which gives them their color and helps them to make their food. This green material is called **chlorophyll**. Without this green material and sunshine, plants cannot make food.

HOW PLANTS MAKE FOOD

STEP ONE

> The leaves drink lots of water. The water comes through the roots, up the stem, and into the leaves.

STEP TWO

> The leaves also take in a special gas from the air. This gas is called *carbon dioxide*.

STEP THREE

> With the help of the sun and the green material, the leaves combine the water and gas (carbon dioxide) which makes a simple kind of sugar and oxygen.

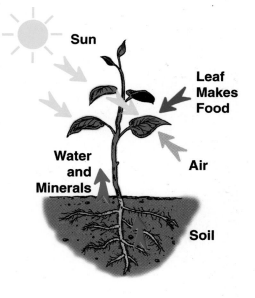

The oxygen goes into the air for us to breathe. Then the food is stored in many parts of the plant. Some foods are stored in leaves like spinach, in stems like celery, in roots like carrots, in seeds like beans and grains, and in fruit like apples. God has given us all these foods to enjoy.

God Made the Herbs

Genesis 1:11 says, "Then God said, 'Let the earth bring forth grass, the herb that yields seed....'" The Bible first talks about grass, which is part of the herb family. Herbs are any plants that grow seeds and have soft stems that dry up after each growing season.

Many people think that herbs are only plants that help our food to taste better or help us to feel better. But herbs include all plants that have soft stems.

Most herbs live only for about six months during the year. When the growing season comes to an end herbs begin to dry up and turn brown. They no longer grow leaves, flowers, or seeds.

Some kinds of vines are part of the herb family. Cucumbers and beans are examples of vines that have soft stems and branches. These vines grow flowers near to the ground. After the bees bring yellow dust (pollen) to the flowers they start to grow into cucumbers or beans.

There are also plants of the herb family that grow tall like trees. Sugar cane is an example of a grass that grows tall—seven to fifteen feet high. It is very sweet to the taste. Bamboo is also a kind of grass that grows so tall that some people call it a "tree" by mistake. Sometimes it grows more than 120 feet high and one foot wide! Bamboo is so strong that it can be used for building houses, bridges, and furniture.

God Made the Trees

God made trees that yield fruit that contains seeds. Some of these seeds will grow into new trees. Trees are plants that live many years and produce a lot of wood in their stems and branches. These plants have one tall stem made of wood. They stand straight without anything holding them up.

Most trees have six parts: (1) large, strong roots; (2) one tall, straight stem called a trunk; (3) branches that grow out of the main stem or trunk; (4) a crown or "bushy head" made of leaves; (5) flowers that grow in springtime; and (6) fruit which comes in all shapes and sizes. God made these wonderful plants for us to enjoy and use in many different ways.

WHY GOD MADE THE TREES

God made the trees so we can enjoy their great beauty. Have you ever seen a cherry or apple tree filled with flowers in the spring? Trees also help us to breathe! The leaves take in gas (carbon dioxide) from the air and change it into another gas called oxygen. It is a special gas which we need to breathe.

We can also use trees for food. Fruit trees give us sweet things to eat like peaches, oranges, dates, and kiwis. Nut trees give us crunchy things to eat like walnuts, cashews, and pecans. Spice trees give us cinnamon and nutmeg. Trees give us medicine like quinine to help stop malaria. Trees are useful in building homes and making paper, as well.

Thank God for all the useful things that trees do for us. God is great and is to be greatly praised.

CROWN

BRANCHES

TRUNK

ROOTS

55

God Made the Leaves

God made most leaves flat and wide, but some trees have leaves that look like needles. As we studied earlier, grasses have long leaves that are narrow (not wide). These are the three main kinds of leaves.

Most leaves are made up of two parts: the blade and the leafstalk. The blade has "veins" or tiny tubes that carry food and water throughout the blade. These veins also help to make the leaf strong.

SIMPLE LEAVES

The leafstalk is like a "handle" that connects the leaf to a stem or branch. The leafstalk also has "veins" that move food and water in and out of the leaf. Some plants like grasses do not have leafstalks. Their blades are wide at the bottom; this wide part wraps itself around the stem to hold it up.

COMPOUND LEAF

56

Activity

One way to enjoy God's beautiful creation is to collect several kinds of leaves from trees. Plan a field trip to a local park or forest preserve to pick one leaf from each kind of tree. Maybe your neighbor has different kinds of trees in his yard. Always remember, however, to ask if it is alright to pick leaves from them.

VEINS

BLADE

When you start collecting tree leaves you will find that there are two main groups in the forest— simple and compound. A simple leaf has only one blade on every leafstalk, but a compound leaf has more than one leaf on every leafstalk. See how many you can find of each group near your home or at a local park.

STALK

After you have collected several leaves, bring them home to dry. Put them between sheets of wax paper and press them in big, heavy books until they are completely dry. After they are dry, glue (use rubber cement) the dried leaves on separate sheets of paper, write their names next to them, and put the papers into a three-ring binder.

For a book cover, you may want to do a crayon rubbing of some of the leaves. Place the leaves upside down so the veins of the leaves are facing up. Then cover them with a sheet of paper and rub a crayon over the leaves. The lines of the veins will appear. Now you have a beautiful rubbing of your leaves for your cover.

Looking Back

Questions

1. What did God divide on the third day of creation?
2. Why did God create the dry land and the seas?
3. What two things are found in soil?
4. What are the three main kinds of rock?
5. What is a common mineral that we use on food?
6. Name the four oceans.
7. Name two families of plants that God formed.
8. Name the three parts of the seed of a corn plant.
9. Name the two parts of a leaf.

Matching

mineral	deep cuts
currents	salt
trench	paths of the sea
narrow	"grains"
seeds	not wide

Fill in the blank

1. Minerals are things that come from

   _____.

2. The _____ is the outer layer of the earth.

3. _____ rock is made from hot liquid rock that comes from volcanoes.

4. _____ rock is made from tiny bits of rock that are pressed hard by water.

5. _____ rock is sometimes made under great heat and pressure.

6. The oceans are filled with _____ water.

7. _____ are plants which have soft stems.

8. _____ are plants which have hard stems.

DAY 4

God made the Sun, Moon, and Stars

Then God said, "Let there be lights in the firmament of the heavens to divide the day from the night; and let them be for signs and for seasons, and for days and years; and let them be for lights in the firmament of the heavens to give light on the earth"; and it was so.

Then God made two great lights: the greater light to rule the day, and the lesser light to rule the night. He made the stars also. God set them in the firmament of the heavens to give light on the earth, and to rule over the day and over the night, and to divide the light from the darkness. And God saw that it was good. So the evening and the morning were the fourth day.

— Genesis 1:14–19 —

The Sun Rules the Day

On the fourth day of creation, God created lights in the sky to separate the day from the night. One of these is the sun, which is a big bright ball that shines on the earth during the day. The sun gives us light so that we can see. The sun also gives light to help make plants grow.

The sun is very big. It is larger than a million earths put together. Why, then, does the sun look so small? Because it is very far away. How does a big airplane look when it is flying high in the sky? It looks small like a toy airplane. In the same way, the sun looks small because it is about 93 million miles away from the earth!

When it is daytime, the sun gives us light, but you cannot see the sun shine all the time. It only shines on one half of the earth at a time. When the sun shines on our part, it is day; and when it is night, it shines on the other part.

Activity

For this activity all you need is a flashlight. Pretend that the flashlight is the sun. As you shine it on different objects you will see dark places, or shadows, behind each object. Why do the shadows appear? This is what the sun does when it shines on the earth. A shadow appears when the sunlight is blocked by an object.

WARNING! The sun is very bright. You should NEVER look directly at the sun; it could hurt your eyes. If you stare at the sun, even with sunglasses, you will become blind!

The Moon Rules the Night

God also put lights in the sky to rule the night. At night, it is often dark outside, but if there are no clouds, you may see the moon and stars. The moon is very bright and the stars may even twinkle, but where did the sun go? The sun is still shining, but it is shining on the other side of the earth. It also shines on the moon and makes it very bright. This means it is daytime on the moon. One day on the moon is equal to 30 days on the earth!

The moon is very different than the earth. The moon is smaller and it does not have any air or water. Could you live very long on the moon without them? No, you need air and water to live. It also is very hot on the sunny side of the moon and very cold on the dark side of the moon!

Activity

If you have a globe, place it at one end of a table and a stack of books at the other end. Darken the room. Place a flashlight on the stack of books. Shine the flashlight directly on the globe. Does the light create a shadow? Yes, the globe blocks the light of the flashlight like the earth blocks the light of the sun.

Now set a grapefruit on a tall glass near one side of the globe. Sit facing the dark side of the globe with the grapefruit to one side. Do you see the flashlight? No, but you see light from the flashlight shining on one side of the grapefruit. This is the same way the moon gets its light from the sun.

God Made the Stars

On a clear night, if you look up into the sky you can see the stars. These stars are huge "suns" that God placed very far away from Earth. You cannot see all of them with your eyes; but with the help of a telescope, you can see many more. Do you know what a telescope is? It is a long round tube with a piece of glass at each end of the tube which make the stars look bigger and much closer.

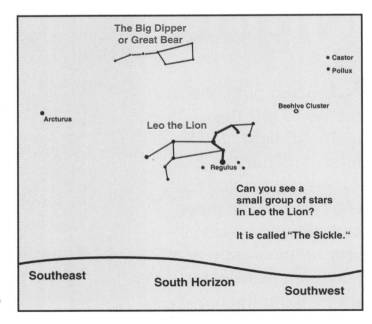

God has put some of the stars into groups. The Bible says that God gave names to each group of stars. Some look like animals—the "Great Bear," "Lion," and "Big Dog." Some look like people—the "Herdsman," "Twins," and a mighty hunter called "Orion" (Job 9:9, 38:31). There are two groups of stars that look like big soup spoons—the "Big and Little Dippers."

If you lived in Australia, southern Africa, or South America, you would see a beautiful group of stars called the "Southern Cross." It can be seen every day of the year from these continents.

Activity

If you have a telescope, go outside at night and look up in the sky. What do you see? Try to find some of the star groups that you studied. If you have a book on stars from the library, it will help you to find them.

Do you know what these groups of stars are called? They are called **constellations**. This big word means that these stars are set together in the sky. They usually look like an object, animal, or person.

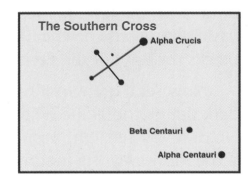

Lights in the Sky

Since God had already created the light, why did He make the lights in the sky? One reason is that God is the Ruler of the heavens and the earth. He wants us and all His creatures to learn that we must obey His will. Even the heavens must obey His commands (Read Genesis 1:14).

Another reason God made the lights in the sky is to show us His glory. The Bible says, "The heavens declare the glory of God; and the firmament shows His handwork" (Psalm 19:1). Do you remember what the word "firmament"

means? It is the heavens above the earth; it reaches high into the sky and goes far beyond the earth, moon, and sun. The firmament is so large that it is hard to think of how big it really is!

We must praise God for His greatness and power which He has painted across the sky. When we look at the sky at night, we see how small and helpless we truly are. God created the heavens above to declare His glory. Stop and pray to our great God and Creator. Thank Him for all He has made for us to enjoy. Ask Him to help you understand the signs and seasons which are set by the sun, moon, and stars.

Signs and Seasons

spring

God made the sun, moon, and stars as signs. These signs tell how long each day is. They also rule the seasons. They determine when it will be summer, when the sun shines more, or when it will be winter, when the sun shines less.

God also made these signs to set the length of each year. A year is divided into four seasons. Each season lasts about ninety days or three months. God has a special purpose for each season. Learn the name of each season—spring, summer, fall, and winter.

summer

fall

winter

64

Spring

Spring comes after the cold winter season. The days begin to get warmer and longer. The earth comes alive after its long winter "nap." God sends rain to help the herbs (plants with soft stems) and trees (plants with hard stems) to grow new leaves and flowers.

Around March 21 in the Northern Hemisphere, spring begins. Spring begins in the Southern Hemisphere around September 22. This is the day when the

daytime is equal to the nighttime. From this moment on, the days get longer and warmer until the beginning of summer.

Spring is the time to plant flowers or a small tree. If you have a garden, help your mom and dad plant some vegetables. Within a few months they will be ready to eat.

Summer

During the summer, the earth is tilted toward the sun more than during the winter. Since the beams of sunlight shine directly on the earth, it warms the earth up. Everyone likes to be outdoors during the summertime. This season of hot, sunny days begins around June 22 in the Northern Hemisphere. Around December 22, the summer begins in the Southern Hemisphere.

God made the summer for a special reason. Plants grow fast in the summer months. Living things need lots of sunshine and water to grow well. If God did not provide summer, the plants would not grow and we would have no food.

Activity

What you need:

bean seeds; potting soil; water; two clear plastic cups

What to do:

Do this activity to learn why the summer sun is so important. Fill both cups half full with potting soil. Do not push down on the soil. Push a few seeds just under the surface of the soil, then add some water. Put one cup in the sunlight and put the other cup in a dark part of your home. Continue to water both when needed. Check them after one week. Which plant looks green and healthy? Which one grew faster? Why?

Fall

Fall is the season when the leaves change color; some turn dark brown, bright yellow, or deep red. Do you know why they change color? In the trees, the sap—which is made up of water and food—stops flowing to their leaves and they dry up. The dried food that is stored in the leaves give them their color. Then the leaves drop to the ground.

The fruit of plants also ripen at this time. We can gather the vegetables from our gardens just like the first Pilgrims did many years ago. This season is a busy time, because food needs to be picked and stored before the cold wintertime begins. This is called the time of **harvest**.

The fall season begins around September 22 in the Northern Hemisphere. Around March 21, fall begins in the Southern Hemisphere. As fall settles in, the earth begins to grow colder and darker. This happens because the earth begins to tilt away from the sun. The sun does not shine as strongly as it did during the summertime. The herbs dry up and die, and many trees lose their leaves and begin their winter rest.

Winter

Winter is a time for God's creation to rest and repair. Many animals sleep all during the winter. The trees and herb plants also rest and wait for spring to come.

During the winter the earth is tilted farthest away from the sun. This is why the days of winter are cold and snowy. In the Northern Hemisphere, the winter begins around December 22, which is the shortest day of the year. Around June 22, winter begins in the Southern Hemisphere. After this time the days become longer.

Winter is a time for cold weather. God sends the snow to cover the earth. This protects most of the plants from the cold, cold weather. Winter is also a time to enjoy the snow and many winter sports.

68

God Rules Over the Seasons

"While the earth remains, seedtime and harvest, and cold and heat, and winter and summer, and day and night shall not cease" (Genesis 8:22).

God created each season for a special reason. The spring brings new life to earth, and the herbs and trees begin to grow after the winter rest. The summer brings the warm sunshine which helps the plants to grow and make many wonderful things to eat. Then comes the harvest with the fall, when the plants begin to die or fall asleep. Finally, the winter lets all of creation rest until spring comes once again.

Activity

What you need:

pictures from magazines, etc.; scissors; glue or rubber cement; poster board; black marker

What to do:

Go through many old magazines and cut out pictures that remind you of the four seasons. After collecting your pictures, glue them on a piece of poster board. You could divide the poster board into four columns or squares with a black marker. Also print the name of each season above its pictures.

Looking Back

True or False: *(Circle the correct answer.)*

1. God gave us four seasons.   True   False
2. Each season lasts one year.   True   False
3. Our seasons are spring, summer, fall, and winter.   True   False
4. Spring is very hot and dry.   True   False
5. Summer is dark and cool.   True   False
6. Fall is the time for raking leaves and picking fruit.   True   False
7. Winter is hot and sunny.   True   False

Matching

     big ball of light   stars

     small ball of light   sun

     huge "suns"   moon

Fill in the blank

1. God made the sun, moon and stars as _____.

2. A year is divided into four _____.

3. In the Northern Hemisphere, March 21 is about when _____ begins.

4. The _____ sun helps plants to grow.

5. _____ change color in the _____ as the sap stops flowing.

6. The shortest day of the year comes around _____ 22 in the Southern Hemisphere.

7. God _____ over the seasons.

Name the four seasons.

                            _____

                            _____

                            _____

                            _____

DAY 5

God Created the Fish and Birds

*T*hen God said, "Let the waters abound with an abundance of living creatures, and let birds fly above the earth across the face of the firmament of the heavens." So God created great sea creatures and every living creature that moves, with which the waters abounded, according to their kind, and every winged bird according to its kind. And God saw that it was good. And God blessed them, saying, "Be fruitful and multiply, and fill the waters in the seas, and let birds multiply on the earth." So the evening and the morning were the fifth day.

— Genesis 1:20–23 —

God Creates Life

On the fifth day of creation, God created something wonderful. It was something that He had not done before. On this day, God created living creatures. The Bible says that the earth was **void** or empty, but then God chose to fill the empty earth with fish and birds.

"Then God said, 'Let the waters abound with an abundance of living creatures, and let birds fly above the earth across the face of the firmament (sky) of the heavens'" (Genesis 1:20). This is the first time that the word "life" is found in the Bible. God filled the earth with sea creatures and birds that fly.

WHAT DID GOD CREATE?

Genesis 1:21 tells us that God created three groups of animals: great sea creatures, living sea creatures, and winged birds. God made each member of these groups on Day Five.

The great sea creatures are very big and long, which include whales, crocodiles, and other large creatures. The living sea creatures include all kinds of fish, clams, snails, starfish, jellyfish, and other unusual animals. Large numbers of these creatures of the sea come in all shapes and sizes.

The winged birds include robins, eagles, ducks, geese, wild turkeys, parakeets, penguins, and ostriches—just to name a few.

1. Great Sea Creatures

The word for "great sea creatures" found in the Bible refers to all kinds of big sea animals that are very long. These large creatures include what we now call whales. Whales are the largest animals in the world.

The largest animal in the world is the blue whale. It is larger than the biggest dinosaur that ever lived. This whale grows to a length of 100 feet and weighs as much as 150 tons!

Another large sea creature is the crocodile. This creature belongs to a group of animals called **reptiles**. The crocodile has a long snout filled with big teeth, webbed feet with large claws, and a powerful tail to help it move in the water.

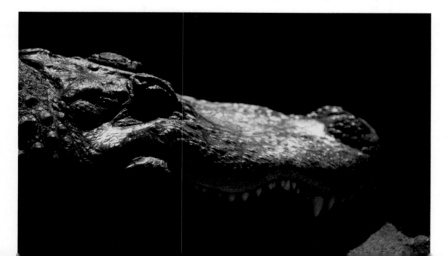

73

2. Living Sea Creatures

God made special kinds of living sea creatures like whales, dolphins, and porpoises that breathe like we do. They have mouths but they breathe through a hole on the top of their heads called a spout. After they swim underwater for a while they have to come to the surface of the water to breathe. This is when you can see such animals, because they blow out the water first and then breathe in the fresh air. They also are different because they do not lay eggs like fish and other sea animals do. They give birth to their babies alive.

Dolphins are beautiful sea animals that can be seen at a special place called an aquarium where they do special tricks for food. Of all the sea creatures that God made, these animals seem to be the smartest.

Color the porpoises at play.

74

Fish with Bones

Did you ever eat fish for dinner. Fish tastes good. God made the fish for us to enjoy. They live in the water. They swim in the oceans, in the lakes, in the ponds, and in the rivers. Fish spend their whole lives in the water. God made them to live there.

God made fish with skeletons. Do you know what a skeleton is? A **skeleton** is the part of an animal that supports its body and protects its important inner parts. God made fish in two different ways. Some fish have skeletons of bone, and others have skeletons of cartilage.

Fish with bones, or boney fish, have skeletons that are made of bones that are either soft or hard. Almost all fish have this kind of skeleton. These include bass, cod, perch, salmon, and tuna.

God gave fish for us to eat: "Whatever in the water has fins and scales, whether in the seas or in the rivers— that you may eat…." (Leviticus 11:9–12). Fish give us energy to run and play and live for God's glory. They also give us vitamins and minerals that help us to live and grow.

75

HOW GOD MADE BONEY FISH

Since God made fish to live in the water, He gave them a special kind of body. Each fish has a big head, gills, fins, scaly skin, and a tail. God made each part of the fish to help it live and move easily in the water.

A fish has an unusual way of breathing. First it drinks some water! After the fish closes its mouth, the water passes through its **gills** and out of its body. Do you know what the gills do? They collect tiny bubbles of oxygen from the water. Fish use these oxygen bubbles to breathe.

A fish also has an interesting way of moving in the water. God created fish with special "feet" and "hands" for swimming. These are called **fins**. Fish swim by moving them back and forth. All fish have fins which come in different shapes and sizes.

A fish also has skin that makes a slime which covers its body and gives off a "fishy" smell. The fish's silvery skin protects it by acting like a mirror— reflecting what is around it. The skin is covered with **scales** that grow in size as the fish gets bigger.

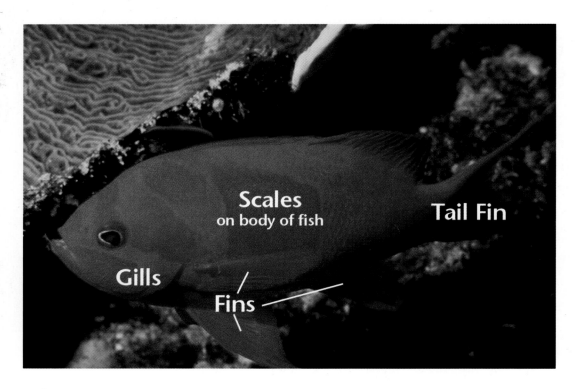

Scales
on body of fish

Tail Fin

Gills

Fins

76

Fish Without Bones

As you learned earlier, God made fish in two different ways. Some fish are boney, and others do not have bones. The fish without bones have a skeleton made of cartilage. Do you know what cartilage is? It is a strong, white material that is springy. Of all the fish that God created, only a few kinds have a skeleton of cartilage.

Sharks are the best known of the fish without bones. Of all the sea creatures, people are most afraid of sharks. Many kinds of sharks have been known to attack people. These fish have mouths called **jaws** which are filled with up to twenty rows of very sharp teeth. When their teeth fall out, new ones grow back.

Another kind of fish without bones is the ray. It swims through the water by moving its large, flat body like large wings. The ray lives mostly on the bottom of the ocean floor, covering its body with the sand. The most dangerous ray is called the stingray. It has a stinger filled with poison at the end of its tail. Stingrays sometimes grow up to seven feet wide.

The largest ray is the giant manta. It grows up to twenty-five feet across and weighs over 3,000 pounds. This huge creature may jump up to fifteen feet out of the water.

Manta Ray

Strange Creatures of the Sea

Conch shell

God also created many other unusual animals that live in the water. Some of them you may have heard about. Others you may have never seen. Yet God made them all. Some of them have shells, and some have no bones or skeletons at all. Others look like plants, while others look like snakes. All of these sea creatures have one thing in common—all of them do have backbones.

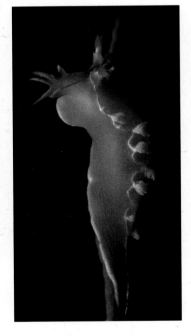

Sea slug

SEA CREATURES WITH SOFT BODIES

One group of these water animals are called **mollusks.** This is the largest group of sea creatures in the world. Each mollusk has only one "foot" that helps to move it along. It does not have a foot like you have, but it has a soft, moist "foot" that helps it move.

Octopus

Some mollusks have an outside skeleton, or shell, to protect them, such as the conch, nautilus, oyster, and certain snails. Others do not have a shell at all; some of these sea creatures are the octopus, squid, and slug.

Squid

SEA CREATURES WITH SPINY SKELETONS

God created another group of sea creatures that do not look like animals at all. They look more like funny-looking rocks or underwater plants. These water animals all have little "needles" or spines that grow out of skeletons which are inside their bodies.

One of these creatures looks like a star. Do you know what its name is? Yes, it is called a starfish. It has five "arms" that look like points of a star. These "arms" are called rays. The bottom of each "arm" or ray has tiny little feet that work like little suction cups. These tiny feet suck so hard on the two shells of the clam that it can pull them apart and eat the soft part of the clam.

Another water animal called the sea urchin looks more like a pincushion instead of an animal. The pinlike spines that grow out of its hard shell protect the sea urchin because its shell is very thin. The spines also help it turn right side up if it gets knocked over by rushing water or another sea creature. The sea urchin lives on the ocean floor and eats bits of plant and animal parts.

One of the most interesting of these creatures looks like a silver dollar. It is called a sand dollar. It also has tiny little spines that grow out of its skeleton, but they are so short that they look like the fur of a land animal.

The Smallest Creatures of the Sea

Some of the creatures that God created do not have skeletons at all. These are the smallest creatures of the sea. Some of them look like worms without rings; some have round, flat, or baglike bodies; some are so small that they are made up of only one cell! Since there are so many kinds of small sea creatures, you will only have time to learn about three of them.

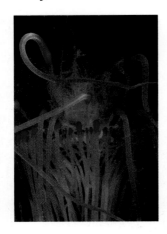

The jellyfish is a beautiful sea creature that has a body that looks like a bowl that floats upside down. It also has long, thin "fingers" that grow on the under side of its body. Beware! These long, fingerlike growths can sting you if you get too close. Their poison can be harmful but it is mostly painful. These "fingers" protect the jellyfish from its enemies and help it to capture food.

The smallest of God's creatures are made up of only one cell. Can you tell what this tiny animal looks like? It looks like a slipper. It has many little body parts. If you look closely you can see that it is covered with very tiny "hairs"; they help it move through the water. The "hairs" near its "mouth" push the food into its body.

Activity

The slipper-like Paramecium

If there is a freshwater pond near to where you live, collect some water and weeds that live in the water. Put them in a jar and let them sit for a couple of days. The jar should be filled with tiny slipperlike creatures within a few days. These freshwater animals are so small they will look like tiny white spots. If you have a magnifying glass or microscope, you can look at them up close. You can tell your friends that you are the proud owner of the smallest pet in the word!

80

3. God Created the Birds

Did you ever spend time watching birds fly? Have you ever wished you could fly like them? God created birds so they can fly fast and far. Flying protects them from their enemies. Do you know how it protects them? Flying helps them quickly get away before their enemies get them.

All birds have wings but not all birds fly. Some birds such as the ostrich, penguin, and kiwi bird can only walk on the ground. Most birds are able to fly, however. Most of these fly close to the ground or up to half a mile high. A few birds can fly over mountains—nearly six miles high!

How God Made Birds

God made each bird with a small, lightweight body and a skeleton made of strong bones. A bird's hard backbone helps it easily move its powerful muscles. A bird even has places in its skeleton for small air sacs which help the bird breathe and make it lighter. God also gave each bird two important gifts that other animals do not have—feathers and wings.

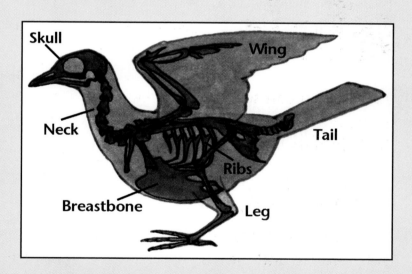

The feathers are lightweight for flying, and yet they keep the bird warm high in the cold air. God made feathers in a special way to help them fly. The second gift is wings. Different kinds of birds have different kinds of wings—some for flying high, some for gliding and diving, some for flying a long way, and some for flying fast. Some birds, such as penguins, have wings for swimming!

BEAKS

Birds have hard covers over their mouths that are called **beaks** and **bills**. God made birds with different kinds of beaks—each kind for gathering a special kind of food. A hawk has a sharp bill that looks like a hook, which helps it to kill and cut its food. A woodpecker has a long, chisel-like bill that helps it find insects that live in the bark of trees. A sparrow has a short, stubby bill for eating seeds. A hummingbird has a long, thin bill for sucking nectar from red flowers.

FEET

Birds also have special kinds of feet. For example, the duck spends a great amount of time in the water. Because of this, God gave the duck webbed feet. Why do you think this is so? Webbed feet help the duck to swim in the water. Most birds have four toes, three in the front and one in the back to keep them steady. The ostrich is the only bird that has only two toes.

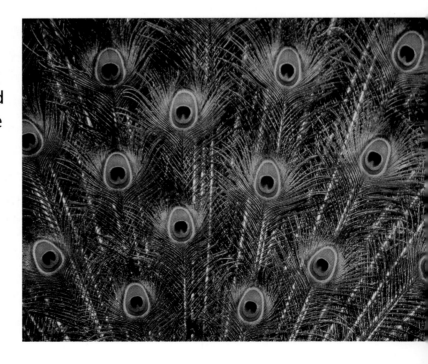

TAILS

God also made birds with beautiful tails such as the peacock with its colorful, fanlike tail. God made the dove with a long, pointed tail; the starling with a short, square tail; the barn swallow with a forked tail; and the mockingbird with a perfectly rounded tail. God made each kind of tail to help these birds to fly better.

82

Water Birds

God has given most water birds webbed feet for swimming, feathers to keep water off their bodies, and a flat beak for catching fish. Ducks and geese like to clean their feathers with oil. They straighten, clean, and oil their feathers with their beaks. Their oily feathers not only keep water off their bodies, but also trap air close to their sides helping them to float in the water.

The graceful swan is one of the most beautiful birds in the world. It uses its broad beak and long neck to find food. The swan sticks its head, neck, and half of its body under the water to catch fish, frogs, and animals with shells.

Some water birds—like cranes, egrets, flamingos, herons, and storks—do not have webbed feet. They are not needed because these birds walk around in shallow water looking for food. God gave them long necks to reach down into the water to catch their food.

The flamingo is one of the most unusual looking birds; it has a bent beak, a long neck, and skinny legs. The feet of this pink bird are wide so they do not sink into the mud as it eats. After the flamingo captures its food, it wags its head from side to side in the water filtering out its food. It always lives with a huge number of other flamingos.

83

Birds That Hunt

Golden Eagle

God has given some birds the ability to fly very fast and see other animals from far away. Many of these kinds of birds are hunters. Instead of feeding on bugs, they eat other small animals. Have you ever seen a hawk soar high in the sky? Have you ever heard an owl hoot in the night? Have you ever seen the great bald eagle? If you have, you have seen hunter birds.

The eagle is one of the most majestic birds that hunts for food. Some eagles can spot food from over five miles away. The golden eagle has wings that are over six feet across. It hunts over mountain clearings or more open areas of the forest. In the rain forest, the harpy eagle hunts for small birds, monkeys, sloths, and snakes, killing them with its sharp claws.

The desert is the home of one of the fastest birds in the world—the falcon. Its feathers keep it cool during the day and warm at night. The fastest animal in all the world is the peregrine falcon, which lives in the forests of the northern hemisphere. From 5,000 feet up in the air, this falcon swoops down on its food and kills it with a single blow. It can reach speeds of 200 miles per hour!

Activity

Plan to visit a local zoo. Do you know what a zoo is? Yes, it is a place where people go to see many wild animals up close. It usually has a bird house where you can see many of the birds you have studied. If you take your book with you, look for these birds.

You could also plan to visit an aquarium. Do you know what an aquarium is? It is a special place that has big tanks of water which hold fish and other kinds of sea creatures. Be sure to take your book with you, so you will be able to find some of the animals you learned about in this chapter.

Winter Vacation

"Look at the birds of the air, for they neither sow nor reap nor gather into barns; yet your heavenly Father feeds them" (Matthew 6:26). Our great Creator takes care of even these small animals— during the winter, spring, summer, or fall.

Wintertime is very cold in certain parts of the earth. At this time, many people like to take a vacation to where it is warm. Many animals do the same thing. When you are outside playing in the snow, do you ever see a swallow? No, because they have gone on vacation. They fly away to where it is warm, and they can find more food. This is called migration.

In the spring, however, the swallow is quick to return because it is warm again. This vacation is a gift that God has given not only to swallows, but to monarch butterflies, whales, and many other animals. Without it many of these animals might starve to death.

Canada gueese flying south
for the winter

"Even the stork in the heavens knows her appointed times; and the turtledove, the swift, and the swallow observe the time of their coming…" (Jeremiah 8:7).

God in His wisdom created each of these birds with a special "clock" inside. It tells them when to fly to warmer climates and when to return home.

Barn Swallow

85

Looking Back

Questions

1. What did God choose to fill the earth with?
2. What is the largest animal in the world?
3. What is the part of an animal that supports its body?
4. List three parts of a fish.
5. What animal has a long snout filled with big teeth?
6. How do whales, dolphins, and porpoises breathe?
7. Name the two ways that God made fish skeletons.
8. How do fish breathe?

Matching

hunter bird	empty
breathing hole	bald eagle
migration	spout
void	winter vacation

Fill in the blank

1. The _____ has wings six feet across.

2. Ducks and geese like to _____ their feathers with oil.

3. Most water birds have _____ feet for swimming.

4. Birds' _____ are lightweight for flying and help to keep them warm.

5. Fish without bones have skeletons made of _____.

DAY 6

God Made the Land Animals and Man

Then God saw everything that He had made, and indeed it was very good.

THEN GOD SAID, "Let the earth bring forth the living creature according to its kind: cattle and creeping thing and beast of the earth, each according to its kind"; and it was so. And God made the beast of the earth according to its kind, cattle according to its kind, and everything that creeps on the earth according to its kind. And God saw that it was good.

THEN GOD SAID, "Let Us make man in Our image, after Our likeness; let them have dominion over the fish of the sea, over the birds of the air, and over the cattle, over all the earth and over every creeping thing that creeps on the earth." So God created man in His own image; in the image of God He created him; male and female He created them.

THEN GOD BLESSED THEM, and God said to them, "Be fruitful and multiply; fill the earth and subdue it; have dominion over the fish of the sea, over the birds of the air, and over every living thing that moves on the earth." And God said, "See, I have given you every herb that yields seed which is on the face of all the earth, and every tree whose fruit yields seed; to you it shall be food. Also, to every beast of the earth, to every bird of the air, and to everything that creeps on the earth, in which there is life, I have given every green herb for food"; and it was so.

THEN GOD SAW everything that He had made, and indeed it was very good. So the evening and the morning were the sixth day. — **Genesis 1:24–31** —

A. God Made the Land Animals

On the sixth day of creation, "…God made the beast of the earth according to its kind, cattle according to its kind, and everything that creeps on the earth according to its kind. And God saw that it was good" (Genesis 1:25). Our Creator made three more groups of animals: beasts of the earth, cattle, and creeping things.

1. Beasts of the Earth

The largest animals belong to the group called the beasts of the earth. These include the wild animals that roam freely over the face of the earth. God made elephants, lions, tigers, bears, giraffes, and dinosaurs. God made all of these animals in one day, and not over a long period of time like some books say.

2. Cattle

The second group includes the cattle—all kinds of farm animals. God made the cow, ox, sheep, and goat on the sixth day. This group also includes the camel, llama, and other animals used to carry people and goods. Many four-legged animals are part of this group—water buffalo, yak, reindeer, moose, and elk.

3. Creeping Things

The third group of animals that God made on this day are the creeping things. These are the smallest animals that move either with or without feet. Some are so small that they are hard to see at times. Small reptiles, amphibians, insects, and worms all make up things that creep upon the earth.

1. God Made the Beasts of the Earth

On the sixth day of creation, God made the beasts of the earth. These are the large wild animals that live on the land. The beasts of the earth are made up of two different groups of animals—reptiles and mammals.

LARGE REPTILES

The first group of beasts is the reptiles. The word **reptile** means "creeping" thing. Reptiles are cold-blooded animals that have backbones and hard pieces of skin on their bodies. Their young are hatched from eggs.

The largest reptiles no longer live on earth. They probably died either during the Great Flood or shortly after it. Do you know what these large reptiles are called? They are called dinosaurs. The word **dinosaur** means "terrible lizard."

Do you know what dinosaur was the largest? The brachiosaur was the largest one that God made. It was about seventy feet long, forty feet tall, and weighed eighty-five tons—the same as ten elephants! With its long neck, it ate the leaves on the trees. God was wise in the way He made the dinosaurs.

Activity

Cut out pictures of animals from old magazines as you learn about them. You may want to trace pictures of them from library books; then cut out the traced animals and color them. Now glue the pictures you found on a plain sheet of paper. Write the name of each animal below its picture. Your first page will be about dinosaurs. Each new page will have a different group of animals on it.

LARGE MAMMALS

The second group of beasts is the mammals. The word **mammal** comes from the word "mamma" or "mother." Mammals are warm-blooded animals that have backbones and some hair on their bodies. Female mammals give milk to their "babies." These beasts of the earth include elephants, giraffes, and zebras. There are so many, however, that you cannot learn about all of them in just one book!

The Elephant

Do you know what animal has big ears and a long nose? Yes, an elephant. God made two kinds of elephants—one kind lives in Africa and the other in Asia. The African elephant is the largest land animal in the world. It is twenty feet long, thirteen feet high, and weighs up to eight tons. Its two ivory tusks can weigh about 250 pounds each. It also has a six-foot trunk that weighs 300 pounds!

God gave the elephant a long trunk for a special reason. The elephant uses its trunk to smell, drink, and grab food. Since the elephant eats leaves and small branches from trees and tall grasses, it uses its trunk to grab this food and put it in its mouth. It also can suck water up its trunk and spray into its mouth for a drink.

God was wise in the way He made the elephant's trunk.

The Giraffe

Another interesting animal is the giraffe. Do you know how tall it grows? It can grow eighteen feet high! It is the tallest of all living animals. Why did God give the giraffe a long neck? He gave it a long neck to reach its favorite food—leaves from the acacia and mimosa trees. The giraffe also has two horns on top of its head and one between its eyes. Its spotted coat helps it hide in the shade of trees.

The Hippopotamus

God also made the hippopotamus—the second largest land animal in the world. It weighs about four tons! Do you know what its name means? It means "river horse." This is a good name because it likes the water. It enjoys living in the water so much that it can still see and breathe while it is almost completely under water. God gave it special eyes and a nose that stick up out of the water.

Activity

Don't forget to cut out pictures of an elephant, giraffe, and hippopotamus from old magazines. Glue these pictures to a new sheet of paper and write the name of each animal below its picture. If you have a folder or notebook, you can keep all your papers together. Name your folder.

THE HORSE FAMILY

The horse is a mammal that has been very helpful to people for thousands of years. Since it is very fast and strong, the horse has been used to help men fight in wars, carry heavy loads, pull wagons, plow fields, and, in 1860, to deliver mail from Missouri to California. Now it is used mostly for horseback riding, horse racing, and rodeo shows or contests.

Horses come in all sizes. The large Clydesdale of Scotland grows to be more than 2,000 pounds, while the small Shetland pony weighs less than 200 pounds. All horses, however, have only one toe on each of their four "feet" or hoofs. God also gave them powerful legs for galloping and strong teeth to eat lots of their favorite food—grass. Horses also can smell and hear very well.

The donkey is also part of the horse family, but it is smaller than the horse. The donkey has long ears, thin legs, small hoofs, and makes a loud, hard cry. The mule is the close relative of the donkey and the horse. It is large like a horse but has a shorter head, long ears, and cries like a donkey.

92

Unusual "Horses" of Africa

The zebra is one of the most interesting members of the horse family. Do you know what makes it so interesting? It has black and white stripes on its coat. This "striped horse" grows to be about eight feet long, five feet tall, and weighs nearly 800 pounds. God made it very fast so it can run away from lions and leopards which try to eat it for lunch! The zebra does not like to eat other animals—only grass and leaves from small bushes.

The most unusual member of the horse family does not even look like a horse. Most horselike animals have only one toe on each foot, but this unusual animal has three toes. Also, have you ever seen a horse with horns? Well, this large animal has two horns—one long pointed horn at the tip of its nose and one large horn on the top of its head between its eyes. It weighs over 6,000 pounds! Do you know its name? It is called a rhinoceros.

Activity

Cut out pictures of a horse, donkey, zebra, and rhinoceros from old magazines. Glue these pictures to a new sheet of paper and write the name of each animal below its picture. Add it to your folder or notebook.

Color the rhinoceros picture at left.

93

THE CAT FAMILY

Do you have a pet cat? What is its name? God made the smallest kitten to the largest animal in the cat family— the tiger. Tigers are big jungle cats that live in India. All cats have good hearing. They can hear sounds that people cannot hear! God also gave them very good eyes because they like to hunt for food just when the sun begins to set. Can you see well when it gets dark?

Tigers are the largest and most powerful animals in the cat family. They like to live in the forest, but they have been found everywhere from the cold tundras of Siberia to the hot jungles of Malaysia. Some stand four feet tall and nine feet long, not including their three-foot tails. Some weigh over 500 pounds! Tigers like to eat all kinds of animals. They use their powerful claws to grab their food.

Lions are big cats that like to roar. Can you roar like a lion? They are found in India and central Africa. Lions like to live in the open plains. They are smaller than tigers, standing only three feet tall and eight feet long. Father lions have large furry manes that cover their heads and light brown fur. Each father lion watches over his family. Do you know what his "family" is called? Yes, it is called a **pride**.

Activity

Cut out pictures of cats from old magazines. Glue these pictures to a new sheet of paper and write the name of each animal below its picture. Add to your folder or notebook.

94

THE DOG FAMILY

The grey timber wolf is a wild member of the dog family. It grows to be more than six feet long, three feet tall, and weighs up to 175 pounds. It lives mostly in the Arctic areas of Asia, Europe, and North America. Can you find where it lives on a map or globe? It also travels in a group called a **pack**. Do you know how it "talks"? It howls and makes other noises.

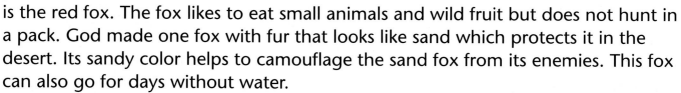

The smallest member of the dog family is the fox, which weighs only about fifteen pounds. The most common fox in the world is the red fox. The fox likes to eat small animals and wild fruit but does not hunt in a pack. God made one fox with fur that looks like sand which protects it in the desert. Its sandy color helps to camouflage the sand fox from its enemies. This fox can also go for days without water.

Some members of the dog family make wonderful pets. Do you have a pet dog? What is its name? Dogs have a good sense of hearing and smelling which makes them useful for tracking animals, hunting game, guarding property, searching for the lost, and herding livestock. Dogs can even guide blind people as they walk. Most of all, dogs make the best friends.

Activity

Cut out pictures of dogs from old magazines. Glue these pictures to a new sheet of paper and write the name of each animal below its picture. Add it to your folder or notebook.

THE BEAR FAMILY

Do you have a fuzzy stuffed bear? It probably looks like the big bears that live in Asia, Europe, and North America. The largest bear in the world is the Alaskan brown bear. It lives on or near Kodiak Island, so it is sometimes called a Kodiak

bear. Can you find where it lives on a map? It may grow more than ten feet long and weigh up to 1,700 pounds! It is closely related to the grizzly bear, so beware! This fuzzy brown bear may seem friendly, but it becomes angry very easily and may even hurt people.

All bears have large heads, long noses, and stubby tails. They walk on four short legs that are very strong. Instead of feet, they have paws; each paw has five toes with one big claw on each toe. Bears also have long, fuzzy fur that hangs loose on their bodies. They have a hard time seeing and hearing but no problem smelling. They use their noses to look for food. Bears like to eat many kinds of food, both plants and animals. God also gave them powerful jaws and strong teeth to eat their food.

Activity

Cut out pictures of bears from old magazines. Glue these pictures to a new sheet of paper and write the name of each animal below its picture. Add it to your folder or notebook.

96

MAMMALS THAT LIVE IN TREES

Primates are mammals that live in trees. These animals include apes, which do not have tails, and monkeys, which have tails. All primates have hands that grasp, five fingers on each hand, and nails instead of claws on each finger. God made them this way so they can easily move in the trees, hold things up close to see, and eat with one hand. Primates have hair all over their bodies.

Some people say that man is a primate, but man is different from the animal kingdom. The Bible clearly states that man was created in the image of God and was given a living soul. God created man to love and obey Him with all his heart, soul, mind, and strength (Mark 12:30). This is why man is different from the animals. In fact, God commanded man to rule over the animal kingdom.

Gorilla "toddler" exploring his surroundings

Apes

The great apes include the gorilla and chimpanzee, which are found in Africa. The gorillas, the largest of the primates, grow to be six feet tall and weigh up to 400 pounds! Male gorillas live on the ground and walk on all fours, but the females and young ones live in the trees and build nests for sleeping. They spend most of the day looking for food except when they take their afternoon nap.

Adult male
Mountain Gorilla

Chimpanzees are also great apes that live in the jungles of Africa. They only weigh about 125 pounds and like to eat fruit, nuts, and small animals. Chimpanzees live in large groups of 40 or more chimps, but when they look for food they go in groups of four or five. They like to eat from sunrise to sunset, except in the heat of the midday sun when they travel on the ground or rest in the trees.

Monkeys

One group of monkeys lives in the warm places of Africa and Asia. They walk on all fours and can grasp things in their "hands" and "feet." These monkeys may weigh as little as five pounds or as much as the 100-pound baboon. God gave them pouches in their cheeks so they can store food. He also gave them pockets in their stomachs which help change the leaves they eat into food.

Another group of monkeys lives in the warm places of Central and South America. They have thin arms and a long tail which they use like a "fifth hand." These monkeys can hold things with their "feet" but not with their "hands." They may weigh as little as two ounces or as much as the twenty-pound howler monkey. The owl monkey is the only monkey in the world that is active at night.

Activity

Cut out pictures of apes and monkeys from old magazines. Glue these pictures to a new sheet of paper and write the name of each animal below its picture. Add it to your folder or notebook.

Color the monkey hanging from the branch.

98

MAMMALS THAT EAT INSECTS

Large Anteaters

Anteaters are mammals which eat ants and do not have any teeth. The giant anteater of Central and South America grows to be six feet long, including its long, bushy tail, and weighs up to fifty pounds. It has a long, round nose and a long tongue that sticks out nearly two feet! The anteater uses its strong claws to dig up ants, termites, and beetle "babies" which are called **grubs**.

The aardvark lives in Africa and looks like a pig with large rabbit ears. Do you know what aardvark means? It means "earth pig." It grows to be seven feet long, has a two-foot tail, and weighs about 130 pounds. It uses its short, thick legs and long claws to dig into ant hills, so it can eat ants and termites with its long, sticky tongue. It is very shy and comes out only at night to eat.

Bats

Bats are mammals that have winglike "arms" which help them fly. The small bats are the ones that like to eat insects. They weigh about an ounce or less and have a wingspan of about six inches. Bats make their homes in caves, hollow trees, and wherever there is a small place to hide. When at home, they like to rest hanging upside down.

Activity

Cut out pictures of a giant anteater, aardvark, and bat from old magazines. Glue these pictures to a new sheet of paper and write the name of each animal below its picture. Add it to your folder or notebook.

The "Flying Fox" (fruit-eating) bat sleeps upside down.

99

LARGE RODENTS

Do you know which family mice and rats belong to? They belong to the rodent family. This large family is made up of 2,000 different kinds; and they all have one thing in common—they like to gnaw. Do you know what **gnaw** means? It means

to "bite down on" something, over and over again. All rodents have two pairs of teeth in the front of their mouths used for gnawing; one pair is on the top jaw and one is on the bottom. Rodents have hair all over their bodies except for their tails.

The Porcupine

The porcupine is a big rodent that has stiff, sharp hairs that stick out of its back. These "hairs" are called **quills**, or **spines**. The muscles on the porcupine's back make the quills stand up to protect it from its enemies. This rodent grows to be about two feet long and weighs up to forty pounds. Did you know that it lives in trees? It likes to eat bark, buds, twigs, and leaves.

The Groundhog

The groundhog, or woodchuck, is the largest member of the squirrel family. Even though it is a "squirrel," it likes to live on the ground. It grows to about two feet long, not including its bushy tail, and weighs about fourteen pounds. The groundhog likes to eat plants, but sometimes it will eat snails and insects. During the winter, it digs a hole in the ground and "sleeps," or **hibernates**.

Activity

Cut out pictures of a porcupine and groundhog from old magazines. Glue these pictures to a new sheet of paper and write the name of each animal below its picture. Add it to your folder or notebook.

MAMMALS OF AUSTRALIA

Mammals That Have Pouches

Have you seen a kangaroo or a koala before? They belong to special group of mammals called **marsupials**. This big word means mammals with "pouches," or "pockets"; these pouches are used for carrying their babies. These mammals may be as small as the marsupial mouse, which is only a few inches long and weighs less than half an ounce, or as large as the great gray kangaroo, which is eight feet long and weighs more than 150 pounds. Their babies are born blind and without hair.

Most marsupials are found in Australia or on nearby islands. The kangaroo is the best known marsupial because of its large back legs and strong tail on which it hops. Some can jump as high as thirty feet and travel thirty miles per hour. Baby red kangaroos stay in their mother's pouch up to eight months. There are more than fifty kinds of kangaroos, including the smaller wallabies or the larger wallaroos.

The koala is another marsupial that looks like a fuzzy gray bear with a large head and hairy ears. The koala grows to about three feet long and weighs about thirty pounds. It likes to eat the leaves of eucalyptus trees. The wombat is another marsupial that likes to dig holes in the ground. The numbat is a marsupial anteater with white stripes on its back. It looks a little like a rabbit with a long tail.

Opossums are the only marsupials outside of Australia. They are found in North and South America.

Activity

Cut out pictures of a kangaroo, koala, and opossum from old magazines. Glue these pictures to a new sheet of paper and write the name of each animal below its picture. Add to your folder or notebook.

THE RABBIT FAMILY

Have you ever held a rabbit? It is a soft, gentle animal. The rabbit family is made up of eighteen members, including rabbits, hares, and pikas.

Rabbits and Hares

Rabbits and hares are different. Rabbit babies are born blind, hairless, and helpless; but hare babies are born seeing, hairy, and strong—hopping shortly after birth. Beware! The names of these animals may be confusing. For example, a jack<u>rabbit</u> is a **hare** and the Belgium <u>hare</u> is a **rabbit**!

A rabbit's coat is usually brown or gray. The short-eared rabbit from Sumatra, however, has stripes of brown and gray on its body with a reddish bottom. Do you know what male and female rabbits are called? Male rabbits are called **bucks**; females are called **does** and are usually larger than the bucks.

Activity

Cut out pictures of a rabbit and hare from old magazines. Glue these pictures to a new sheet of paper and write the name of each animal below its picture. Add it to your folder or notebook.

Color the jackrabbit.

102

Looking Back

Questions

1. What does the word "dinosaur" mean?
2. What is the largest land animal in the world?
3. What is the tallest living animal?
4. What does "hippopotamus" mean?
5. What member of the horse family has black and white stripes?
6. What unusual member of the horse family has two horns?
7. Name the largest animal in the cat family.
8. What is a father lion's family called?
9. What is a group of wolves that travel together called?
10. What is the largest bear in the world called?

Matching

mammal	primates without tails
monkeys	earth pig
aardvark	bite down on
apes	"mother"
gnaw	primates with tails

Fill in the blank

1. The _____ _____ is the only monkey that is active at night.

2. _____ are mammals that have winglike "arms" which help them fly.

3. The _____ is a big rodent that has stiff, sharp hairs called quills.

4. An animal that _____ is one that "sleeps" all winter.

5. The largest member of the squirrel family is the _____.

6. Mammals that have pouches for carrying their young are called _____.

7. Male rabbits are called _____, and female rabbits are called _____.

2. God Created the Cattle

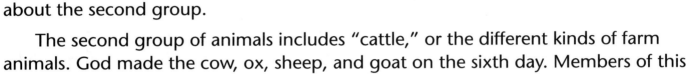

On the sixth day of creation, as you know, "…God made the beasts of the earth according to its kind, cattle according to its kind, and everything that creeps on the earth according to its kind. And God saw that it was good" (Genesis 1:25). You have already studied many in the first group of animals— the beasts of the earth. You will now learn about the second group.

The second group of animals includes "cattle," or the different kinds of farm animals. God made the cow, ox, sheep, and goat on the sixth day. Members of this group are sometimes used to carry people and goods; they include the camel, llama, and other such animals. Many four-legged animals are also part of this group, such as the water buffalo, yak, reindeer, caribou, moose, and elk.

All the animals in this group chew their **cud**. Cud is the food that cattle have eaten and put in their first stomach. The cud then comes up from the first stomach and they chew it again. God was wise when he made cattle, because they need to chew their food a couple of times before they can digest it. Cattle also grow horns or antlers and have an even number of toes on each foot.

104

THE COW FAMILY

Members of the cow family are called **bovids**. They include bison, buffaloes, yaks, antelopes, cows, sheep, and goats. All bovids grow hollow horns, but the horns of the antelope look more like deer antlers. Most antelopes live in Africa and can run fast. They include the gnu or wildebeest, kudu, and sable antelope.

American Bison

Large Bovids

Bison are wild bovids that include the American buffalo and the European wisent. Bison stand over six feet tall and may weigh over 2,000 pounds! They are known for their large heads and shoulders which are covered with long, shaggy hair. Wisents are a bit larger than the American buffalo but look more like cows.

Wild bovids also include the Asian water buffalo and the African buffalo. Their horns are not round like other bovids, but have three flat sides; they grow up to fourteen feet across. Water buffaloes are so gentle that even children can lead them. African Cape buffaloes, however, can be very dangerous.

Yaks are wild bovids that live in the mountains of Tibet. Yaks stand about six feet tall and weigh 1,200 pounds. They can climb mountains, are good swimmers, and like to eat grass. Their shaggy hair hangs almost to the ground. Tibetans use them for milk, meat, leather, and cloth; they are also used to carry heavy loads.

Color the Cape buffalo.

105

Small Bovids

God created cows to help people in many ways. Some cows are raised for their milk or meat, while others are bred to produce both milk and meat. In the United States, most beef cows are bred in Texas, Nebraska, Kansas, and Iowa; most dairy cows are raised in Wisconsin, California, New York, and Pennsylvania.

Sheep are smaller bovids that also have hollow horns. Found all over the world, farm-raised sheep are used for their wool and meat. In Iran, however, the skins of lambs are sold as fur; and in China, cheese made from sheep's milk is sold as a common food. Sheep oil is also used in lotions and creams.

Goats are like sheep because they have two toes on each foot and they chew their cud. The hair of goats is different, though. Beautiful mohair and cashmere clothing is made from their hair. Goats are mostly raised for their milk and meat. They like to eat grass, shrubs, leaves, and twigs.

Activity

Cut out pictures of a buffalo, yak, cow, sheep, and goat from old magazines. Glue these pictures to a new sheet of paper and write the name of each animal below its picture. Add it to your folder or notebook.

THE DEER FAMILY

The deer family is found almost all over the world. They are the only animals that grow antlers. Deer antlers are made of solid bone—not hollow like the horns of the cow family. Only the male members of the deer family grow antlers, except for female reindeer which also grow them. Some deer do not grow any antlers.

Moose and Elk

The largest member of the deer family is the North American moose. It stands nearly eight feet tall and weighs almost 2,000 pounds! The moose has a piece of skin, called a **bell**, hanging from the bottom of its head. Its large antlers look like wide "platters" with stubby fingers on top of them.

The American elk is the second largest member of the deer family. It likes to eat grass, twigs, leaves, and other plant parts. The elk grows five feet tall and weighs almost 1,000 pounds. Its five-foot-wide antlers alone weigh about fifty pounds!

Caribou and Reindeer

Caribou and reindeer are the only members of the deer family where both the males and females grow antlers. Caribou are larger than reindeer and stand about five feet high and weigh more than 650 pounds; reindeer stand only four feet tall and weigh only 250 pounds.

Activity

Cut out pictures of a moose, elk, caribou, and reindeer from old magazines. Glue these pictures to a new sheet of paper and write the name of each animal below its picture. Add to your folder or notebook.

THE CAMEL

There are two kinds of camels—the dromedary and the Bactrian. The dromedary camel has one hump and lives in the Middle East. It has been used for thousands of years for travel, milk, meat, wool, hides, and fuel from dried dung. It stands seven feet tall and weighs 1,500 pounds. The Bactrian camel comes from Central Asia, has two humps, and is a little smaller than the dromedary.

The camel is a mammal that chews its cud and has two padded toes on each foot. Its feet are not split like other members of the "cattle" group, because there is a piece of skin between its two toes. God wisely made the camel's feet so it can walk easily on the sand. God also gave the camel long, thick eyelashes and a nose that closes partly to keep out the sand that blows in the desert.

The camel was created to live in very hot places. God made the camel so it can go without water a long time. It does not get thirsty because it gets water from the plants it eats in the desert. The camel keeps so much water in its body that it can go for months without drinking! When it does get thirsty, it can drink up to 300 gallons of water in a short time without getting sick.

Activity

Cut out pictures of a dromedary camel and Bactrian camel from old magazines. Glue these pictures to a new sheet of paper and write the name of each animal below its picture. Add it to your folder or notebook.

Color the camel above.
Can you tell what kind it is?

Looking Back

Questions

1. What large bovid is so gentle that even children can lead it?
2. What are the only animals that grow antlers?
3. What animal can drink up to 300 gallons of water at a time, when it gets thirsty?
4. What kind of oil is used in lotions and creams?
5. What are farm-raised sheep used for in different parts of the world?
6. Which kind of camel has one hump? Two humps?

Matching

bison   goats hair

mohair   members of the cow family

bovids   wild bovids

Fill in the blank

1. The second group of animals God created on Day 6 is called _____.
2. All bovids grow _____ horns.
3. Yaks are wild bovids that live in the mountains of _____.
4. The largest member of the deer family is the North American _____.
5. Most _____ _____ are raised in Wisconsin, California, New York, and Pennsylvania.
6. _____ is the food that "cattle" have eaten and put in their first stomach to chew later.

Small Bovids

Name three kinds of small bovids:

   1. _____

   2. _____

   3. _____

109

3. God Created the Creeping Things

On the sixth day of creation, "…God made the beasts of the earth according to its kind, cattle according to its kind, and everything that creeps on the earth according to its kind. And God saw that it was good" (Genesis 1:25). This verse tells us that our Creator made three groups of animals: the beasts of the field, cattle, and creeping things. You will now learn about the third group.

On Day 6, God made the creeping things. These are the smallest animals that move either with or without feet. Some are so small that they are hard to see at times. Some can only be seen through a microscope, a special tool that lets us see tiny creatures. The things that creep upon the earth include small mammals, small reptiles, amphibians, insects, and earthworms. God made so many creeping things that all of them cannot be included in this book!

THE WEASEL FAMILY

The weasel family is made up of animals with long, thin bodies and short legs. They are very busy mammals that never seem to rest. Weasels are found almost all over the world. Weasels include the mink, ermine, polecat, ferret, marten, and wolverine. The fur of the mink, ermine, and wolverine, is made into beautiful coats.

The badger, otter, and skunk are also members of the weasel family. The badger has a wide, flat body; small head; and short legs. It can dig fast and fight hard with its big, heavy claws. It grows to be about three feet long and weighs up to twenty-five pounds. It usually lives on the ground, but some like to live in trees. It eats gophers, mice, ground squirrels, and other small animals.

The otter is found almost all over the world. God gave it webbed feet so it can swim in the water. The otter grows to about three feet long, not including its tail, and weighs up to thirty pounds. It likes to eat sea creatures, birds, and other small land animals. The sea otter likes to eat and sleep while floating on its back!

The skunk is a weasel which has black fur with white stripes down its back. It is the only weasel that can spray its musk two feet away. The strong smell of the musk protects the skunk from its enemies. It grows about two feet long and weighs about three and one half pounds. It eats plants and small animals.

Activity

Cut out pictures of a badger, otter, and skunk from old magazines. Glue these pictures to a new sheet of paper and write the name of each animal below its picture. Add it to your folder or notebook.
.

111

SMALL RODENTS

As you learned earlier, mice and rats belong to the rodent family. They all have one thing in common—they like to gnaw, or to bite down on something, over and over again. All rodents have two pairs of teeth in the front of their mouths used for gnawing; one pair is on the top jaw and one is on the bottom.

Mice and Rats

Mice are found all over the world. They have long bodies, pointed noses, ears that stand up, and tails with little or no hair. Mice often have diseases that they pass on to people; these diseases can make them very sick ; some people even die from them.

Mice of North and South America include the vole, pocket mouse, jumping mouse, and many other kinds. The white-footed or deer mouse is the most common. Mice of Africa, Asia, and Europe include common house mice and field mice. They like to eat plants and insects.

Rats are rodents that look like mice, but they are larger. They also carry diseases that can make people sick. The black rat is the one that caused many people to die in Europe during the 1300s. It grows to about seven inches long, plus its seven-inch tail, and weighs about half a pound.

Color the mouse
in the slab of cheese.

112

Other Small Rodents

Many children like to keep small rodents as pets. The guinea pig and hamster are the most common. The guinea pig grows to be about a foot long and weighs about two pounds. It lives about eight years. The hamster is a bit smaller and uses pouches in its cheeks to store or carry food. It likes to dig long tunnels in the ground which farmers do not like. Do you know why? It ruins their crops.

Squirrels also belong to the rodent family and are a bit larger than a rat. They include chipmunks, woodchucks, and all kinds of squirrels. The gray and red squirrels are the most common tree squirrels. The flying squirrel has large flaps of skin between its front and back legs which helps it to glide in the air.

Other small rodents include the gopher and prairie dog. Gophers like to make many tunnels under the ground which form an underground village. The prairie dog also likes to make tunnels and to live in groups called **coteries**.

Activity

Cut out pictures of a mouse, rat, guinea pig, hamster, squirrel, chipmunk, woodchuck, gopher, and prairie dog from old magazines. Glue these pictures to a new sheet of paper and write the name of each animal below its picture. Add it to your folder or notebook.

SMALL REPTILES

Reptiles are cold-blooded animals. This means they become hot or cold by their surroundings. If they lay in the sun, they will become hot; if they sit in an icy cave, they will become cold. Reptiles also have scales on their skin which help to keep water away from their bodies.

Snakes

Snakes are reptiles that do not have any legs. There are thousands of kinds of snakes in the world, and they eat only small animals. They are very helpful because they like to eat rodents. Snakes live mostly in the warmer parts of the world, but certain kinds are found in the Arctic or in the mountains where it is cold. If it gets too hot or cold, snakes go into a deep sleep.

Most snakes are less than one and a half feet long, but some, such as the python and anaconda, are longer than thirty feet. God gave most snakes eyes that are covered with special eyelids, which are always "closed" so they can protect their eyes. If their eyelids are closed, how can they see? They are clear!

Snakes eat fish, amphibians, reptiles, birds, and small mammals. They find their food by seeing or smelling it. Then some snakes kill their **prey** (an animal hunted by other animals for food) by squeezing it with their jaws and body so it cannot breathe. Others use the poison in their saliva to kill their food. Some snakes use poison in their **fangs** (large, hollow front teeth) to kill their prey.

114

Lizards

Lizards are similar to snakes because both are covered with scales. Lizards are different from snakes because lizards have legs and eyelids that open and close. Most lizards live in the warmer parts of the world. They like to eat fish, tadpoles, other sea creatures, insects, worms, other small animals, and plants.

Lizards grow from only a few inches to ten feet long. They have strong legs, and some can even stand up and run on their back legs! They can move up to nineteen miles per hour. Their skin is dry and scaly. Some can make their skin lighter or darker; chameleons can even change the color of their skin to help them hide from their enemies.

Turtles

Another member of the reptile family is the turtle. It has a hard shell covered with scales around its body. It may be as small as the little bog turtle or as large as the 2,000-pound leatherback turtle, which grows to eight feet long! Turtles do not have teeth, but the sharp edges of their jaws are used to chew their food. The turtle is mostly found in southeastern Asia and southeastern North America.

Activity

Cut out pictures of snakes, lizards, and turtles from old magazines. Glue these pictures to a new sheet of paper and write the name of each animal below its picture. Add it to your folder or notebook.

AMPHIBIANS

God created an interesting group of animals that are born in the water but are able to live on land! These animals are called **amphibians**, and they are cold-blooded. Amphibians have smooth skin without scales, breathe with gills when they are born, and lay eggs. Amphibians are found all over the world except in Greenland and Antarctica.

Frogs And Toads

Frogs and toads are the largest group of amphibians. They live in deserts, water, rain forests, and mountain meadows. These amphibians may be shorter than an inch or as long as three feet like the giant African Bullfrog. Frogs have big heads, webbed feet, and large back legs. They use their back legs to jump, hop, swim, dig tunnels, or climb.

Most kinds of frogs lay many eggs at one time. After they hatch, their babies, or **tadpoles**, start to swim. When they grow up, they become frogs and may live on land. When frogs are in danger, they warn other frogs with a special warning call. Some frogs bend their backs up, become stiff, and rock back and forth on their bellies. Others flash bright colors at their enemies to scare them away.

Toads have fat bodies with short legs. They can walk or hop—but not jump. They are all less than a foot long and have thick, dry skin that is covered with "warts" on their backs. Toads protect themselves with poison that is in pockets on their backs. Their poison hurts the eyes, nose, and throat of their enemies. Most toads live on land and are active at night. They like to eat insects or small creatures.

116

Salamanders

Another group of amphibians include the salamanders. They are found mostly within the warm parts of Asia, Europe, and North America. They live in ponds, streams, and rivers, and, at times, stay under leaves, logs, or rocks where there is a little moisture. They may be as short as one half inch or as long as six feet like the giant salamander of Japan.

The salamander has a short body with a tail, four legs, and a big head compared to the rest of its body. Its smooth skin may be a bright brown, black, yellow, or red. God also gave it good eyes and ears. The salamander likes to eat insects, worms, and other small creatures. Some salamanders live to be sixty years old!

Activity

Cut out pictures of frogs, toads, and salamanders from old magazines. Glue these pictures to a new sheet of paper and write the name of each animal below its picture. Add it to your folder or notebook.

117

INSECTS

Insects are the largest group of animals in the world. Some people say that there are three million kinds of insects! All insects have three parts to their bodies—a **head, thorax** (or middle part), and **abdomen** (end part). There are six legs joined to the thorax, or middle part of its body. They are found all over the world, except in the very cold parts of the Arctic and Antarctica.

The Amazing Grasshopper

The grasshopper is an insect that lives mostly in rain forests, dry areas, or grasslands. Its color is green or brown, and it may have yellow or red marks. God gave it large back legs for leaping and wings for flying. It may grow over four inches long. The grasshopper likes to eat plants, but only a few kinds of grasshoppers ruin crops as they did in Bible times (Exodus 10:1–20; Joel 1:1–12, 2:1–11).

The Southeastern Lubber Grasshopper can be brightly-colored or quite dull in its appearance.

The grasshopper has two sets of eyes! It notices light with its three simple eyes, but it sees through its two compound eyes. Do you know what a compound eye is? It's one of the two big eyes on the grasshopper's head. Each compound eye has hundreds of lenses that help it see. God wisely created the grasshopper with compound eyes so it does not need to move its head to see in all directions.

INSECTS WITH WINGS

Praying mantis

There are nearly thirty groups of insects, but less than ten of these groups have wings. Insects with wings include the grasshoppers and crickets, dragonflies and damselflies, bugs, cicadas and aphids, lacewings, butterflies and moths, beetles, ants and bees, and flies.

Straight-winged Insects

The first group of winged insects have "straight wings"; they hold them straight along their bodies when they are not flying. This group includes the grasshopper, cricket, katydid, and locust—insects that jump. It also includes the cockroach, praying mantis, and the walking stick (*see page 87*)—insects that run.

They like to eat all kinds of plants, especially crops that farmers plant. The praying mantis is the only member of this group that feeds only on other living insects.

Dragonfly and Damselfly

Another group of winged insects includes the dragonfly and damselfly. They have long, thin bodies, two large eyes, and two sets of clear wings. The dragonfly and damselfly cannot walk so they do almost everything in the air!

Green Darner dragonfly

The strong dragonfly can fly up to sixty miles per hour, but the damselfly is a weak flyer. When at rest, the dragonfly holds its wings out flat, but the damselfly holds them straight up and down.

Circumpolar Bluet damselfly

119

Bugs

Bugs are insects which have wings that lay flat on their backs. When at rest, the wings cross over each other and look like the letter "X." God gave them a special mouth part that lets them drink their food like you drink from a straw. They include three large groups—water bugs, land bugs, and bugs that swim on top of the water but live on land.

Giant Water Bug

Cicada

The cicada belongs to another group. It rests its wings in the shape of the letter "A" on its back. The wings look like the roof of a house. One kind of cicada lives underground for seventeen years, feeding on tree roots. Then it comes out for a few weeks, plants its eggs, and dies. Most North American cicadas make fast ticking or buzzing noises, but others make a musical "song."

Activity

Cut out pictures of a grasshopper, dragonfly, water bug, and cicada from old magazines. Glue these pictures to a new sheet of paper and write the name of each animal below its picture. Add it to your folder or notebook.

A cicada has just emerged from its pupal case and is drying its wings before its first flight.

120

Butterflies and Moths

STAGES IN
THE LIFE CYCLE
OF THE BLACK
SWALLOWTAIL
BUTTERFLY

1. *egg is laid on the food plant (wild carrot)*

2a. *caterpillar feeds on the plant leaves*

2b. *caterpillar anchors itself to pupate*

3. *caterpillar sheds its skin and pupates*

There are more than 100,000 kinds of butterflies and moths all over the world. They have wings covered with tiny scales; these scales overlap like shingles on a roof. Butterfly wings are very colorful, but moth wings are mostly dull. God gave butterflies and moths a special nose that acts like a straw; they use their noses to suck sweet "juice" from flowers.

4. *pupal case splits and adult butterfly emerges and dries its wings*

The butterfly or moth goes through four stages of complete metamorphosis. First, it lays its small, hard **eggs.** Second, caterpillars, or **larvae** (babies of the butterfly or moth), hatch from the eggs and feed on plants. Third, the caterpillars turn into **pupas,** also called **chrysalises,** (many moths also spin a covering around their bodies called a cocoon). Fourth, the pupas hatch, turning into adult butterflies or moths.

Activity

Cut out pictures of butterflies and moths from old magazines. Glue these pictures to a new sheet of paper and write the name of each animal below its picture. Add it to your folder or notebook.

121

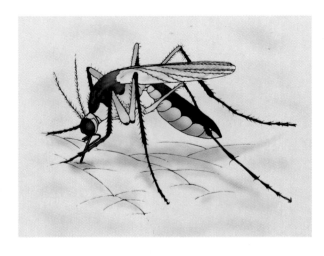

Other Flying Insects

Another group of winged insects is flies. These two-winged insects include the housefly, gnat, and mosquito. These pests walk over all kinds of dirty things and carry germs and sickness. Mosquitoes sometimes carry diseases in their saliva.

Did a mosquito ever "bite" you? When it "bites," the mosquito's saliva goes into your skin. The saliva helps the mosquito sip blood through its long, thin nose. Do you know what makes a mosquito "bite" itch? The saliva makes it itch.

The beetle is part of another group. It is the largest group of animals in the world. The beetle has a special set of wings that cover its body; it meets along a straight line down the middle of its back. These wings are for protection—not flying.

This group includes the dung beetle, June bug, ladybug, boll weevil, and firefly. Most boys and girls like the firefly, or lightning bug, because of its soft, green light that flashes on and off. At night, they are fun to catch and put in a jar.

The last group of insects with wings include the ant, bee, and wasp. They like to live in large groups, or colonies. Each colony is divided into smaller groups that have special jobs—some gather food, some guard the colony, and others help in the nursery caring for the "baby" insects.

The Bible says to go and study the ant and become wise because it is such a hard-working little creature (Proverbs 6:6).

Activity

Cut out pictures of a fly, gnat, mosquito, beetle, ant, bee, and wasp from old magazines. Glue these pictures to a new sheet of paper and write the name of each animal below its picture. Add it to your folder or notebook.

OTHER SMALL CREATURES

Eight-legged Creatures

Another group of small creatures is called the **arachnids**. They include spiders, daddy longlegs, mites, ticks, scorpions, and horseshoe crabs. Arachnids differ from insects in many ways:

Arachnids	Insects
only one or two body parts	three body parts
eight legs	six legs
only simple eyes	simple and compound eyes
eat only other animals	eat plant food
do not have wings	have wings

Spiders may be very tiny or grow up to be more than three inches long. Spiders live everywhere on land and like to eat insects. All spiders have poison, but only the black widow and brown spider may harm people. Spiders also spin silk webs to catch their food.

A black-and-yellow Argiope spider eats its prey (a Giant Swallowtail butterfly).

Another interesting arachnid is the daddy longlegs, or harvestman, which looks like a spider but is different in many ways: the harvestman has one body part, but the spider has two; it has only two simple eyes, instead of eight; the harvestman cannot spin a web like the spider; it eats both plants and insects, but the spider eats only insects.

The scorpion is one of the most dangerous arachnids.

123

Creatures with Hundreds of Legs

Giant Desert Centipede

God created animals that have many legs. One kind is called the centipede. It has a flat body which is divided into many parts, or **segments**. Each segment has one pair of legs attached to it; it may have up to 300 legs all together. The centipede also has two long "feelers" called **antennae** and uses poison to kill its food. It likes to eat toads, small snakes, insects, spiders, slugs, and earthworms.

Rainforest Millipede

Another kind of animal that has many legs is the millipede. It has a round body that is also divided into segments with legs attached to it. It may have up to 400 legs all together. The millipede also has antennae, but they are shorter than the centipede's. They like to eat dead and rotting bits of plants.

Activity

Cut out pictures of spiders, daddy longlegs, centipedes, and millipedes from old magazines. Glue these pictures to a new sheet of paper and write the name of each animal below its picture. Add it to your folder or notebook.

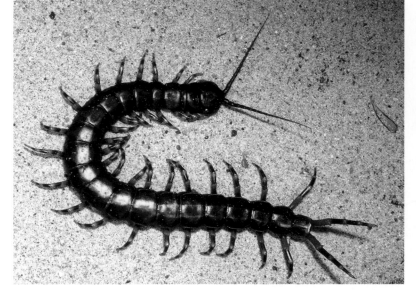

Gigantea Centipede

Looking Back

Questions

1. What is the third group of animals that God created on the sixth day?
2. Which weasel likes to eat and sleep while floating on its back?
3. What rodents carry diseases that are harmful to people?
4. Which two kinds of rodents do children commonly like to keep as pets?
5. Which two kinds of animals are cold-blooded?
6. Name the members of the largest group of amphibians.
7. What is the largest group of animals in the world?
8. What insect rests its wings in the shape of the letter "A" on its back?

Matching

prey	large, hollow front teeth
harvestman	antennae
feelers	frog babies
fangs	animal hunted for food
tadpoles	daddy longlegs

Fill in the blank

1. The _____ is a weasel with a wide, flat body; small head; and short legs.
2. The _____ has black fur with white stripes down its back and sprays musk.
3. The three parts of an insect's body are the _____, _____, and _____.
4. _____ are not insects because they have one or two body parts, eight legs, and two simple eyes.
5. The _____ is an insect that can fly up to sixty miles per hour.

Metamorphosis

Name the four stages of growth that most insects go through:

1. _____

2. _____

3. _____

4. _____

125

B. God Made Man

God also made the first people during Day Six. If you look at people, you can see that they are like mammals in many ways. Mothers, of course, give milk to their babies after they are born. People are also warm-blooded and have hair like mammals. In fact, people and mammals were created on the same day. Does this mean that people and mammals are the same kind of creature? No!

"Then God said, 'Let Us make man in Our image, after Our likeness'" (Genesis 1:26a). God made man in His image. Notice what this verse says, "Let **Us** make man in **Our** image, after **Our** likeness." What does this mean? This means that God the Father, God the Son, and God the Holy Spirit talked and decided to make man in the image of God. People are a special creation of the Creator!

126

Made in the Image of God

People are made in God's image. This means that the Creator made everyone not only with a body, but with a spirit (Genesis 2:7). Each person was created to know God and worship Him. Animals have "spirits" too, but their "spirits" are not eternal (Ecclesiastes 3:21).

Jesus said that "God is spirit, and those who worship Him must worship Him in spirit and truth" (John 4:23). Only people can worship their Creator—animals cannot. This is what makes animals and people different creatures.

God also said, "… let them have dominion over the fish of the sea, over the birds of the air, and over the cattle, over all the earth and over every creeping thing that creeps on the earth'" (Genesis 1:26). What does **dominion** mean? It means to "rule over" something. God commanded people to rule over the animals. If you live on a farm or have a pet, you rule over animals by caring for them.

People are different from animals because people are created in God's image and are commanded to rule over the animals. Moreover, people are different from animals because God gave them a sense of right and wrong. Animals do not know what is right and wrong, but people do.

Activity

Draw a picture of a pet or farm animal that you own. How do you care for it? Draw a picture of what you give it to eat and drink. If your pet or animal gets hurt, what do you do? Draw a picture of how you help your "friend."

127

Glorifying God

Why do people keep doing what is wrong? The Bible says all have sinned and fall short of God's glory (Romans 3:23). Sin keeps us from doing what is right. Where does sin lead? The Bible says, "For the wages of sin is death …" (Romans 6:23). This means separation from God the Creator forever.

If all people have sinned and sin leads to death, how can people glorify and worship God? Romans 6:23 gives us the answer: "… but the gift of God is eternal life in Christ Jesus our Lord." God sent His Son so that everyone that believes on His name will have eternal life (John 3:16).

Do you believe that you have sinned and fallen short of God's glory? Do you believe that the wages of sin leads to death? Do you believe that God sent His Son to die on the cross to pay for your sins? If so, the Bible says, "if you confess with your mouth the Lord Jesus and believe in your heart that God has raised Him from the dead, you will be saved" (Romans 10: 9). Call on Christ Jesus' name and you will be saved.

Activity

Draw a picture of a cross in the middle of a sheet of paper. Write Romans 6:23 under it. Ask your teacher to help you memorize this verse.

Fearfully and Wonderfully Made

God's crowning work of creation took place on Day Six. That crowning work was God's creation of man. Man was not only made in the image of God, but he was given a wonderful body. As you study the human body, you will learn how great and wise God is. What King David said 3,000 years ago is still true today: "I will praise You [God], for I am fearfully and wonderfully made" (Psalm 139:14a).

God makes each person in a special way (see Psalm 139: 13–16). As a baby grows in his mother's womb, all his body parts are formed in the first two months

of his life. No new parts are added, even though he is only one inch long. The baby continues to grow for seven more months. After the baby is fully grown, he comes out of his mother's womb. What a wonderful miracle!

Activity

Draw a picture of your family—mom, dad, brothers, and sisters. You may also draw pictures of your grandparents. God made each of you in a special way.

129

God's Five Gifts to Man

God made each person in a wonderful way. He gave everyone five gifts to help them live on Earth—eyes to see, ears to hear, a nose to smell, a tongue to taste, and skin to touch. These five gifts show us that the Creator God is wise and great. You will learn more about these five gifts, or **senses**.

God's Gift of the Eye

The eye is a wonderful gift from God. He made it in the shape of a ball. On the outside of the eye, a thick covering protects the eye and lets light enter the **pupil**. The pupil is the opening on the front of the eye that looks like a black dot.

The ring around the pupil is called the **iris**. What color is your iris? (Look at your eye in a mirror.) It helps the pupil to open wider to let in more light; it also helps the pupil become smaller to keep out too much light.

Where does the light go inside the eye? It goes through a **lens**, which helps you see clearly. The lens changes shape. It becomes thicker so you can see things up close; it also becomes thinner so you can see things far away.

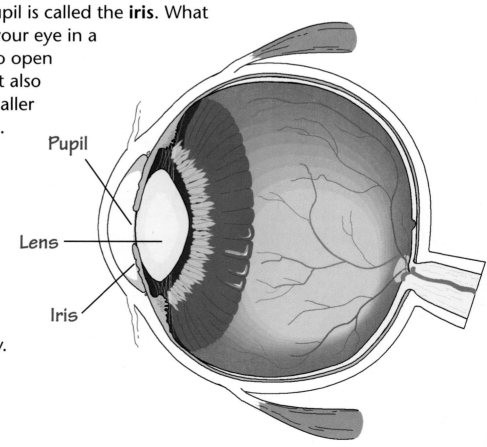

Pupil

Lens

Iris

130

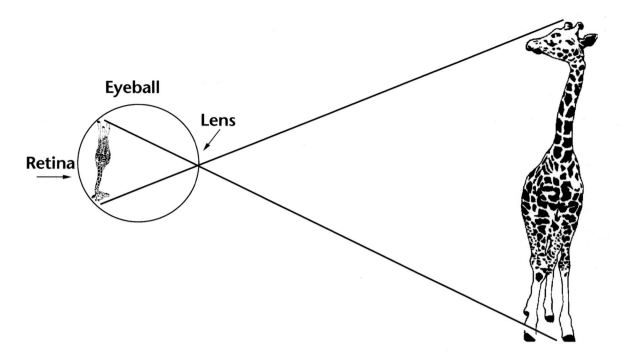

Pretend that you are looking at a giraffe. When the sun shines on the giraffe, the light bounces off the giraffe and goes through the pupil of your eye. Then the lens makes an upside-down picture of the giraffe on the back of the inner eye.

The back of the inner eye is called the **retina**. The retina is made up of millions of cells which take the upside-down picture of the giraffe and send it to your brain. Then your brain turns it right side up!

Activity

Discover how your pupil works. First, look in a mirror and see how big the pupil of your eye is. Now, go to a room in your home where there are no windows and all the lights are turned off. Sit in the room until you are able to see what is in it. After your eyes adjust to the darkness, go look in a mirror and see how the size of your pupil has changed. Is it bigger or smaller? Your pupil is bigger.

If it is a sunny day, go outside. What happens to your eyes? Did you squint a few times? This helps your pupil adjust to the sunlight. Look in a mirror to see how the size of your pupil changed. Is it bigger or smaller? Your pupil is smaller. Why? Since the sunlight was so bright, your eye did not need as much light.

What part of the eye helped your pupil become smaller? The iris made it smaller.

131

God's Gift of the Ear

Another gift God gave to man is the gift of the ear. The ear is divided into three parts—the outer ear, the middle ear, and the inner ear. The **outer ear** is the part that you can see. It catches sounds and sends them through a tube called the hearing canal. At the end of the canal is the eardrum. The sounds hit the eardrum like sticks hit a drum. Even the smallest sound can make the eardrum move.

After the sounds hit the eardrum, they go into the **middle ear**—the ear's "workshop." The eardrum moves three "tools"—the hammer, anvil, and stirrup. These "tools" boost the sounds before they go into the **inner ear**. The stirrup taps on a "window" and the sounds move into the inner ear. Each sound is changed into a tiny signal that goes to the brain. Now you can hear the sounds.

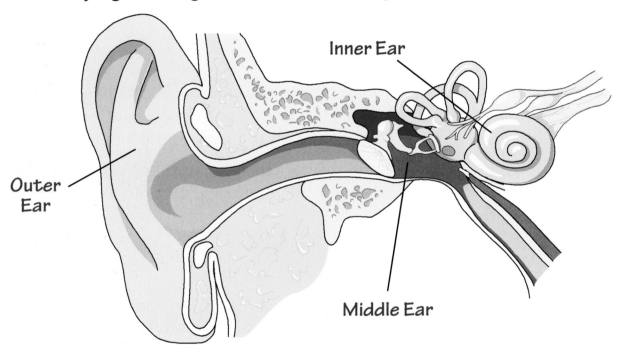

Inner Ear

Outer Ear

Middle Ear

Activity

If you have a conch shell, hold it up close to your ear. (Use a cup if you don't have a shell.) What do you hear? It sounds like the ocean. Do you think an ocean is in the shell? No! You are hearing your blood move through your body. Because of its shape, the shell captures the sounds of your blood moving and sends them back to the ear.

Conch Shell

132

God's Gift of the Skin

The skin is one of the most wonderful gifts that God has given you. It covers all of your body and protects it from many harmful things. Most of all, skin helps you to feel things when you touch them. The tips of your fingers can tell you that the cover of this book is smooth or a rock is rough or cotton is soft. Your fingers can also tell you that an ice cube is cold or that fire is hot.

The skin can also tell you if something is pushing on your body. Can you do push-ups? When you do push-ups, your hands not only feel the floor under you but also the weight of your body pushing down on them. Your skin can feel pain as well. If you fall down while you are running, your skin sends messages to your brain telling you that you scraped your knee or bruised your arm.

Activity

Have your teacher put a blindfold over your eyes so you cannot see anything. Then have your teacher give you different things that are smooth or rough, soft or hard, hot or cold, wet or dry, heavy or light. Name the things you are given and tell how they feel when you touch them.

133

God's Gift of the Nose

The nose is another gift that God gave man. The nose not only helps people to breathe but also to smell. It has two openings called **nostrils**. Air filled with odors enters the nose through these openings.

Then the air and odors fill an empty space, or opening, inside the nose. A small patch of cells on the upper part of this opening catches the odors and sends a message to the brain. This message helps you to smell all kinds of things—flowers, perfume, food, or even a skunk!

The nose protects you from harmful things, too. If you smell food that is rotten, the message sent to your brain tells you that it is not good to eat. If you smell gas or smoke, the message sent to your brain tells you that you are in danger.

God wisely made each person with the ability to smell. God also made the nose to help people taste their food. It tells you what flavor the food has.

Nasal Cavity

Nostril

134

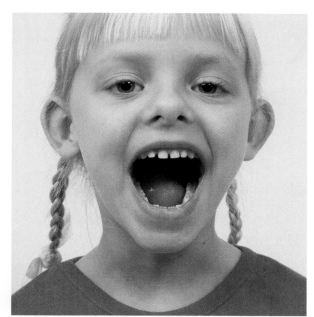

God's Gift of the Tongue

The tongue is a gift from God that everyone enjoys. It has thousands of **taste buds** that tell the brain what kind of food you are eating. These taste buds tell you if the food is salty, sweet, sour, or bitter. Every day these taste buds are replaced with new ones. Without the tongue, you cannot taste food.

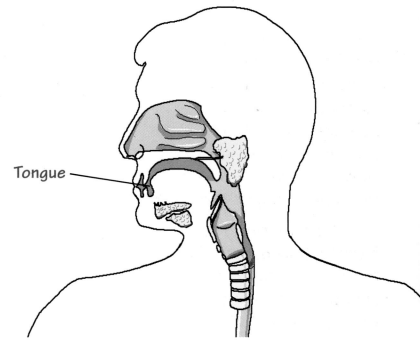

Tongue

The tongue also helps you to swallow your food. After you have chewed your food well, the tongue rolls the food into a small ball, or **bolus**. Then it pushes the ball of food toward the back of your mouth so you are able to swallow it.

God made the tongue to help you talk as well. It helps you make the sounds of all the letters. How many letters in the alphabet are made with the use of the tongue? Yes, all of them. Some groups of letters are also sounded with the tongue, such as the hard and soft sounds of "th" as in *the* and *this*.

Activity

Pick different kinds of food to taste and smell. Take a slice of orange and smell it. It smells fruity. The smell of the orange determines its flavor. Now taste the orange. How does it taste? Yes, it tastes sweet. Now bite into a lemon. What do your taste buds tell you? It is sour, but it smells fruity. If you bite into the peel of a lemon, what will it taste like? It is bitter! Also try salty potato chips.

135

Looking Back

Questions

1. How are people like mammals?
2. How are people different from mammals?
3. Why do people keep on doing what is wrong?
4. Where does sin lead?
5. Whom did God send to bring eternal life to His people?
6. If God saves you, what must you do?
7. What was God's crowning work of creation?
8. What five gifts, or senses, did God give to man?

Matching

pupil   back of inner eye

retina   small ball of food

bolus   opening on front of eye

Fill in the blank

1. The _____ ear catches sounds and sends them to the eardrum.

2. The ring around the pupil of the eye is called the _____.

3. _____ covers your whole body and helps you feel things you touch.

4. After light enters the eye through the pupil, it goes through a _____ which helps you see by changing shape.

5. The _____ tells you what flavor food has.

6. The hammer, anvil, and stirrup boost sounds before they go into the _____ ear.

Name the four things your taste buds tell you:

1._____   2._____

3._____   4._____

DAY 7

God Rested

Thus the heavens and the earth, and all the host of them, were finished. And on the seventh day God ended His work which He had done, and He rested on the seventh day from all His work which he had done. Then God blessed the seventh day and sanctified it, because in it He rested from all His work which God created and made.

— Genesis 2:1–3 —

137

In Six Days

God could have created all things in one moment, but He did not want to do that. He decided to create all things in six days. His example teaches us that we should work six days, and on the seventh day we should worship Him.

Do you help your mom and dad with work around the house? Do you like to build small toys and make things? When you do this, you are working. When you work, you need things to work with, but when the Lord God created the heavens and the earth, He simply spoke. He created the world out of nothing! God is our powerful Creator.

God made everything in six days. He alone is the great Creator, and this is why we praise Him. Stop and praise God for all the wonderful things He has made. Thank Him for making you.

For in six days the Lord made the heavens and earth, the sea, and all that is in them, and rested the seventh day. Therefore the Lord blessed the Sabbath day and hallowed it.

— Exodus 20:11 —

Activity

On a blank piece of paper, draw seven boxes in a row. Write "Day 1" over the first box, "Day 2" over the second box, … all the way to "Day 7" over the seventh box. Draw a picture of what happened on each day of the creation week. On the seventh day, draw a picture of someone praying, singing, or worshiping God. What do you and your family do on the Sabbath?

God Made Everything Very Good

When God finished His work, everything was in perfect order. "Then God saw everything that He had made, and indeed it was very good" (Genesis 1:31). The great Creator God was happy that He made a wonderful world.

Six times before, God saw that what He had made was "good." Now His work was done and everything was "very good." God was very wise in putting the heavens and the earth together. All of creation was beautiful and perfect. There was no sickness, sin, or death. This was how God wanted the world to be—very good.

As God's creatures, we must be sure to worship Him as the great Creator. Thank God for making such a wonderful place for us to live and work and play. Ask Him to help you to obey His word and take care of His world. Because of God's great power and love, we should tell others how He created all things and how they can become a new creation in Christ (Read 2 Corinthians 5:17).

Activity

How do you care for God's world? If you live on a farm or have a pet, you can care for animals by feeding them and giving them water. If you have a garden, you can care for the plants by watering them and pulling weeds. You can also care for God's world by not littering. Do you know what **littering** is? It is throwing paper cups, candy wrappers, or other garbage on the ground instead of putting them in a trash can. On separate paper, list three ways you can care for God's world.

139

Rest on the Sabbath

God wants us to work hard and glorify Him for six days. On the seventh day, however, He wants us to rest from our work and worship Him. He gave us one day to rest from our work like He did when He made all things (Read Exodus 31:17). He gave us this day so that our bodies can rest and we can be refreshed; then we will be able to serve Him for another week.

The seventh day of creation is called the Sabbath. Do you know what Sabbath means? **Sabbath** means "rest." Every Sabbath, you should thank God for everything He has given to you and for the strength to serve Him. It is also good to spend some time alone with God in prayer, thanking Him for your dad, mom, brothers, sisters, grandparents, and friends. Every Sabbath or Lord's Day, you should attend a church that preaches the Bible and worships the Creator God.

Activity

Ask your Dad or Mom to help you create a special "Thankfulness Journal." You can simply begin by writing a short paragraph every Sunday afternoon about one thing that you are thankful God has given you. As each new Sunday arrives, continue to add more and more paragraphs until you create a journal or booklet.

After four months, read your "Thankfulness Journal" to your whole family on a Sunday afternoon.